W9-CKM-507

# KOI OF THE WORLD
## Japanese Colored Carp

by Dr. Herbert R. Axelrod

Distributed in the U.S.A. by T.F.H. Publications, Inc., 211 West Sylvania Avenue, P.O. Box 27, Neptune City, N.J. 07753; in England by T.F.H. (Gt. Britain) Ltd., 13 Nutley Lane, Reigate, Surrey; in Canada to the book store and library trade by Clarke, Irwin & Company, Clarwin House, 791 St. Clair Avenue West, Toronto 10, Ontario; in Canada to the pet trade by Rolf C. Hagen Ltd., 3225 Sartelon Street, Montreal 382, Quebec; in Southeast Asia by Y.W. Ong, 9 Lorong 36 Geylang, Singapore 14; in Australia and the south Pacific by Pet Imports Pty. Ltd., P.O. Box 149, Brookvale 2100, N.S.W., Australia. Published by T.F.H. Publications Inc. Ltd., The British Crown Colony of Hong Kong.

**ISBN 0-87666-092-8**

©1973 by Dr. Herbert R. Axelrod

Original copyright of *The Japanese Colored Carp: Nishiki-Goi* ©1970 by Kodansha Ltd. and original copyright of *Encyclopedia of Nishiki-Goi* ©1971 by Kodansha Ltd., Tokyo, Japan. These books were written by Takeo Kuroki and Tokumitu Iwago.

## ACKNOWLEDGEMENTS

The author is indebted to the Japanese publisher, Kodansha Ltd. for their cooperation in allowing the author the use of many of their magnificent photographs. Many of these photographs appeared in two Japanese books entitled *The Japanese Colored Carp: Nishiki-Goi* which was published in 1970 and the *Encyclopedia of Nishiki-Goi* which they published in 1971. The assistance of Mr. Akira Tazaki who handled the transactions is acknowledged with thanks. Special thanks are due to Mr. Teikichi Tarusawa, Executive Director of Kodansha, who had the wisdom and forethought to envision how beautiful a book his photographs would make if put together into one magnificent volume.

I also wish to acknowledge the great effort of Professor Momozo Kumagai of Keio University. Professor Kumagai took the information about each photograph from the original Japanese sources and translated them into modern English, enabling me to write intelligent captions for the photographs supplied by Kodansha.

Herbert R. Axelrod

# TABLE OF CONTENTS

COVER PHOTOGRAPH: A Kohaku, 53 cm long, weighing 3½ kg, and exhibiting the most perfect form and coloration the author had ever seen (1973).

Title Page: Breeder-sized koi selected for body shape and coloration.

German carp photographed at the Aquarium in Frankfurt, Germany in 1973 by the author. One carp is scaled and one is scaleless.

## A WARNING

In the late 1800's when immigrants from Eastern Europe came to America, they soon realized that even though "the streets were paved with gold," they didn't have any carp in their streams. Carp were a favorite food for many people in Eastern Europe because the fish are so hardy they can be bought alive from local fish markets, insuring their freshness. This was an important consideration 100 years ago, but not today.

So a few thousand baby carp were imported from Germany, raised to maturity, spawned and spread out all over the United States so that anyone could have carp by fishing in their local waters.

At the time this was done people had little idea of the great damage that would ensue. Carp are hardy and can live and breed in water which might be low in oxygen, badly polluted and unsuitable for many other fishes. They are also bottom feeders and continually poke about the bottom of their lake homes stirring up mud and silt so that what was once a clean, clear lake, might now be a muddy one. This silt also deposited upon the eggs of other fishes, suffocating many of them and eventually removing the other species from its lake range because the diminished number of fry could not compete against the increasing numbers of carp.

Japanese colored koi are basically carp with fancy coloration and scalation. They can endure freezing temperatures and at my farm in Florida, they have thrived at a water temperature well into the 90's. So please do not allow your pets to escape into your local waters. Koi are meant to be kept in relatively shallow ponds with concrete or stone bottoms. They should NOT be put into lakes, ponds or any other natural body of water.

Most local laws prohibit the introduction of "exotic" fishes and whilst I was chairman of the Exotic Fishes Committee of the American Fisheries Society, the entire membership of some 5,000 scientists, fishery biologists and fishery management people, voted overwhelmingly in favor of the following "position statement" relative to such introductions.

### Position of American Fisheries Society on Introductions of Exotic Aquatic Species

Our purpose is to formulate a broad mechanism for planning, regulating, implementing, and monitoring all introductions of exotic aquatic species.

Some introductions of species into ecosystems in which they are not native have been successful (e.g., coho salmon and striped bass) and others unfortunate (e.g., common carp and walking catfish).

Species not native to an ecosystem will be termed "exotic." Some introductions are in some sense planned and purposeful for management reasons; others are accidental or are simply ways of disposing of unwanted pets or research organisms.

It is recommended that the policy of the American Fisheries Society be:

1. Encourage exotic fish importers, farmers, dealers and hobbyists to prevent and discourage the accidental or purposeful introduction of exotics into their local ecosystems.

    a. Support legislation prohibiting all ornamental aquarium fish importers, exotic fish importers, hobbyists, breeders, dealers, governmental employees and fish farmers from releasing living, dead or dying fishes into any water system, but encouraging drywells, dikes and moats for the preservation of the ecosystem from accidental introduction of exotic fishes and fish diseases.

    b. Urge the establishment of four Federal Fish Disease and Fish Culture Stations, similar to that already established as the Eastern Fish Disease Laboratory in Leetown, West Virginia, in or near Miami and Tampa, Florida, Los Angeles, California and New York, New York where the majority of exotic fish businesses are located, to assist exotic fish dealers, importers, etc., in the control of fish diseases and the culture and identification of exotic species, and to evaluate, control, and monitor exotic introductions into these areas.

    c. Urge the accurate completion of existing Federal documentation for compliance with Customs and Interior Department regulations. Form 3-177 "Declaration for Importation of Fish or Wildlife" is grossly abused, with deflated costs and generally incorrect information.

2. Urge that no city, county, state or Federal agency introduce, or allow to be introduced, any exotic species into any waters within its jurisdiction which might contaminate any waters outside its jurisdiction without official sanction of the exposed jurisdictions.

5

3. Urge that only ornamental aquarium fish dealers be permitted to import such fishes for sale or distribution to hobbyists. The "dealer" would be defined as a firm or person whose income derives from live ornamental aquarium fishes.

4. Urge that the importation of exotic fishes for purposes of research not involving introduction into a natural ecosystem, or for display in public aquaria by individuals or organizations, be made under agreement with responsible governmental agencies. Such importers will be subject to investigatory procedures currently existing and/or to be developed, and species so imported shall be kept under conditions preventing escape or accidental introduction. Aquarium hobbyists should be encouraged to import rare ornamental fishes through such importers. No fishes shall be released into any natural ecosystem upon termination of research or display.

5. Urge that all species of exotics considered for release be prohibited and considered undesirable for any purposes of introduction into any ecosystem unless that fish shall have been evaluated upon the following bases and found to be desirable:

    a. RATIONALE. Reasons for seeking an import should be clearly stated and demonstrated. It should be clearly noted what qualities are sought that would make the import more desirable than native forms.

    b. SEARCH. Within the qualifications set forth under RATIONALE, a search of possible contenders should be made, with a list prepared of those that appear most likely to succeed, and the favorable and unfavorable aspects of each species noted.

    c. PRELIMINARY ASSESSMENT OF THE IMPACT. This should go beyond the area of rationale to consider impact on target aquatic ecosystems, general effect on game and food fishes or waterfowl, on aquatic plants and public health. The published information on the species should be reviewed and the species should be studied in preliminary fashion in its biotope.

    d. PUBLICITY AND REVIEW. The subject should be entirely open and expert advice should be sought. It is at this point that thoroughness is in order. No importation is so urgent that it should not be subject to careful evaluation.

    e. EXPERIMENTAL RESEARCH. If a prospective import passes the first four steps, a research program should be initiated by an appropriate agency or organization to test the import in confined waters (experimental ponds, etc.). This agency or organization should not have the authority to approve its own results or to effect the release of stocks, but should submit its report and recommendations for evaluation.

    f. EVALUATION OR RECOMMENDATION. Again publicity is in order and complete reports should be circulated amongst interested scientists and presented for publication in the *Transactions of the American Fisheries Society*.

    g. INTRODUCTION. With favorable evaluation, the release should be effected and monitored, with results published or circulated.

Because animals do not respect political boundaries, it would seem that an international, national and regional agency should either be involved at the start or have the veto power at the end. Under this procedure there is no doubt that fewer exotic introductions would be accomplished, but quality and not quantity is desired and many mistakes might be avoided.

Approved by AFS at their Business Meeting
Hot Springs, Arkansas
September 12, 1972

## KOI IN YOUR GARDEN

In Japan where there is so little ground available that a flower garden is physically impossible, people take small areas and 'plant' them with living flowers . . . colored carp. These fishes have been bred for almost 100 years with emphasis placed upon their beauty when viewed from above. The idea and the breeding stock originated in Germany where the Germans bred carp with interesting scales. To this day "German" carp are those with missing scales, or scales which are enlarged and occur in various kinds of odd patterns. The Japanese refer to these carp as "Deutsch" which is pronounced and spelled in Japanese as "Doitsu." The final "u" in Japanese is not enunciated.

So if you are short of space . . . or have too much . . . and you want some year round beauty . . . perhaps some sport . . . perhaps some food . . . consider utilizing Japanese colored carp, or koi as they have become to be known. (The Japanese call them Nishiki-Goi.)

## BASIC NEEDS

Koi are hardy fishes. They can tolerate water that freezes for months providing the water doesn't freeze solid with them inside; or they can take water temperatures which rise to almost 100° providing it does not stay that hot for more than six months. They do require at least a 35° change in temperature to make them fit for breeding (so between 30 and 65° is fine . . . or between 65 and 100° is equally acceptable).

Koi do best in shallow pools with running water. They thrived in my Florida pools which measured about 30 feet square and three feet deep in the center with a slow flow of about 20 gallons of water per hour, 12 hours a day. They also do well in my small pool in New Jersey. This measures about 10 feet by 20 feet, is five feet deep, freezes two feet deep in the winter, gets to 90° in the summer, and only receives an occasional water change two or three times in the summer only. So you can see how well koi tolerate different kinds of temperatures and water conditions.

## FOOD

Koi can be fed almost anything that is small enough for them to swallow and which had an animal or vegetable origin. The best food for them are live foods such as *Daphnia,* but for most of us that's too difficult to collect and too expensive if we have to buy it; I settle for a pelletized food.

If your pond is deep and you want to see your koi, feed them floating pellets. If your pond is shallow, the pellets do not have to float. Fish pellets are available from any petshop, or from your local feed dealer. Trout pellets, chicken pellets (which are basically fish meal anyway), or any fish pellet is fine. I have kept koi for 9 years without feeding them any live foods . . . and this in an isolated outdoor pool where they could scarcely find any natural food. In a pinch, bread will do, but fish pellets are cheaper and better.

Once your fish become accustomed to your feeding them, they can easily be trained to take pellets from your hand. My koi actually stick their snouts out of the water and gobble down handfuls of pellets . . . its fun . . . but watch the family dog and the children! That's why I like shallow pools!

## DISEASES

If you can have running water in your pond, so much the better. Many very successful koi breeders and hobbyists keep their koi pool hooked up to the rain gutter so that every time it rains the koi get a healthy change of water. The excess water goes through an overflow which has a screen top to keep the fish in and to allow the water out.

Water changing is important to the health of the koi. If your koi do not have steady, flowing water, or changes fairly regularly, they often get anchor worm or some other external parasite. These are usually more unsightly than dangerous. My fishes, kept in small ponds in New Jersey, get anchor worm every summer. I have treated them and been rid of them, but it's too dangerous for the average aquarist to treat his pond. The parasites are less dangerous than the treatment!

If you feel up to it, catch your fish and put them into a separate container; drain the pond and have it treated with as much chlorine bleach as you can lay your hands on. About one gallon of bleach for every 50 gallons of pool would be great, but half that is also acceptable. Leave the bleach in the water for an hour, then drain the pond and refill it with fresh water. Put the koi

Children love to feed and play with koi. Teach your child the possible dangers. (Below) The author's favorite koi stretching its head several inches out of the water to be fed.

*Lernaea cyprinacea,* projecting from the skin of the fish, are usual summertime koi problems if you do not have running water.

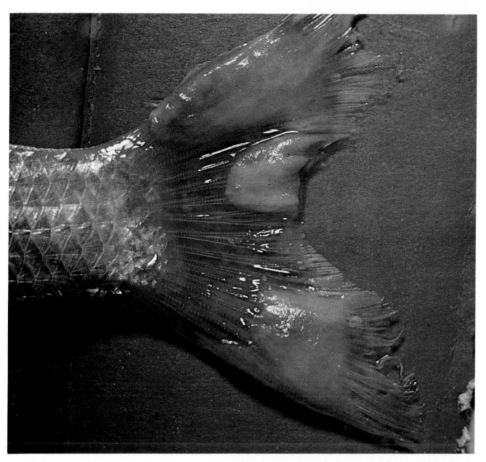

Much more serious than anchor worm is tail rot which has become infected with fungus *(Saprolegnia).* I cut the tail off, painted it with mercurochrome; the fish lived and the tail regenerated.

This German carp has ulcerations which have been caused by dropsy. Photo courtesy of Dr. Reichenbach-Klinke.

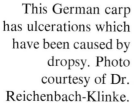

back after allowing the water in the pool or pond to aerate for a day. Be sure to keep your koi in a suitable container while the pond is being cleaned. The container should be aerated with a pump and air stone during the time the fish are crowded. Ask your local aquarium shop for information about pumps and aerators.

Koi get other diseases, but treating them in a pond is very difficult, so you'd best contact your local petshop if he specializes in tropical aquarium fishes or goldfish. Or else, check any one of scores of fish disease books which are available at your local library, bookstore or petshop. The diseases of most fish are the same whether they are trout or guppies . . . or carp. But your carp are much, much stronger and hardier than either guppies or trout. As a matter of fact, they are about the hardiest fish I can think of that has scales.

The two koi ponds on this page are impractical. The pond on the right has no convenient hand-feeding station, while the pond below is green and muddy. On the facing page are two practical ponds.

## PONDS

There are as many different kinds of ponds for your koi as there are different kinds of gardens. It hardly seems necessary to try to describe in words that which can be shown in photographs, so I have selected some of the most typical and beautiful ponds I could find in Hawaii and Japan and have reproduced them here for you to refer to or copy. Almost any large goldfish pool will serve koi well. Small goldfish pools are acceptable to koi, too, but since koi grow larger and larger every year, they may well outgrow the pool! Once you have had koi, and you discover their magnificent beauty and friendliness, you'll probably never look at a goldfish again! Unfortunately that's exactly what happened to me.

So please look at all the beautiful ponds in the accompanying photographs and decide for yourself the kind of pond that will suit you best. Get professional help in making it depending upon your soil, your pocketbook and your idea of beauty . . . but make sure you have a source of water and an overflow apparatus.

Though the Japanese rarely have lotus or water lilies in with their koi, there is no reason why you cannot add some of these beautiful flowering aquatic plants to your own pool.

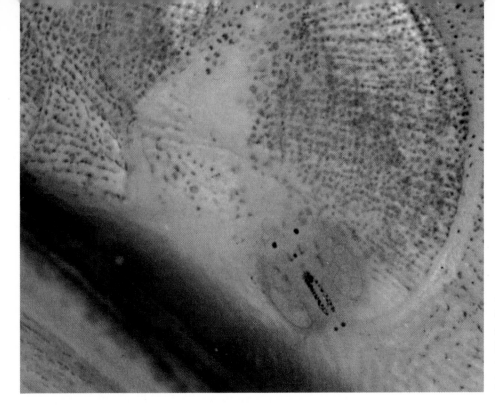

A small carp louse attached to the scale of a koi. This photo is enlarged about 12 times. Photo by Dr. Pierre de Kinkelin.

A carp louse (*Argulus* sp.) enlarged about 50 times natural size. Photo by Dr. E. Elkan.

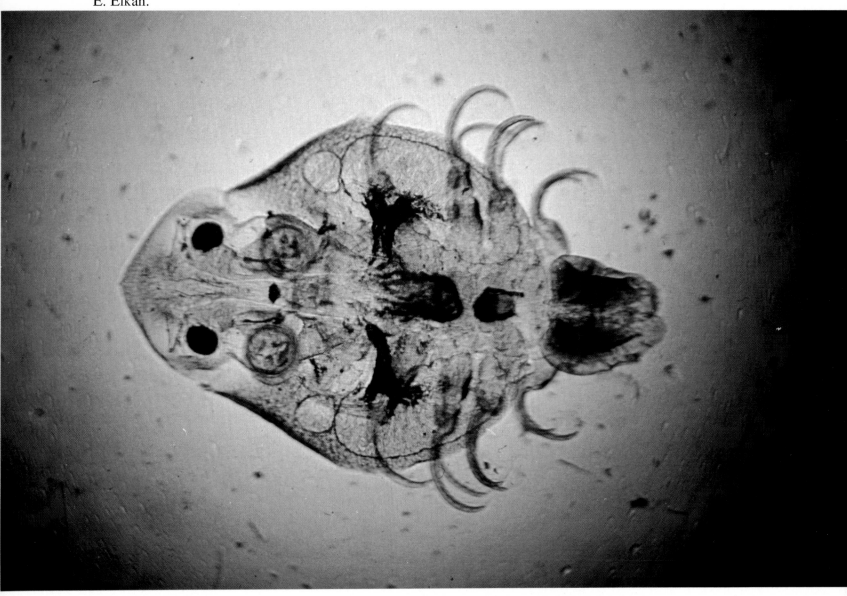

Gill fungus, branchiomycosis, in German carp. Photo by Dr. Pierre de Kinkelin.

A more detailed study of branchiomycosis. Photo by Dr. Pierre de Kinkelin.

A tumor in the carp's side. Photo by Dr. Lionel E. Mawdesley-Thomas.

Carp with ulcers due to hemorrhagic septicemia. Photo by Dr. Pietro Ghittino.

These yearling carp have slight hyperemia of the skin caused by *Aeromonas liquefaciens* infection.

*All of the diseases shown on these two pages are infectious and dangerous (except the tumor). If you see any of these symptoms you must help the koi quickly or you might well lose the whole lot.*

The koi ponds (above and on the facing page) are two of the best the author has ever seen. They have all the characteristics of what I prefer to call a "practical" pond.

A practical pond is one in which the water is maintained in a crystal clear condition by either constant changing or filtration, where the fish can be seen at close range from above, and where the fish can be conveniently hand-fed.

This pool features a lovely small house on stilts, just the thing for feeding the fishes or enjoying a delightful afternoon in the shade. This pool measures 230 m² (about 2800 square feet) in surface area. It has a depth of 70 cm (about 28 inches) and the pool is occupied by about 100 koi measuring from 30 to 60 cm in length.

This koi pool decorates a typical Japanese garden. It has a surface area of 330 m² (about 4000 square feet) and a depth of 70 to 100 cm (28 to 40 inches). The pool has 90 koi which vary in length from 40 to 70 cm.

16

This koi pond is attached to the house allowing the occupants to feed their koi from the porch. The pool measures 43 m² (about 520 square feet) in surface area with a depth varying from 45 to 120 cm (18 to 47 inches). There are 100 koi in the pool which measure from 35 to 75 cm in length.

This beautiful pool measures 33 m² (about 400 square feet) in surface area. It is fairly deep at 150 cm (about 5 feet) and contains 50 to 70 koi from 36 to 60 cm in length. The lovely bridge is a useful feature since it allows perfect overhead view of the fish.

17

This small pool measures only 20 m² (about 240 square feet) and has an average depth of 40 cm (about 16 inches). It contains 250 koi which vary in size from 35 to 80 cm. The pool is fed by almost continuously aerated running water over the water wheel, thus the pool is always clear and can support many large fish.

A handful of floating koi pellets and the fish dash into the center of this 73 m² (883 square feet) koi pool. It is 60 to 150 cm deep (24 to 60 inches) and contains 10,000 koi from 20 to 50 cm in length. There are too many fish here but with heavy filtration and constantly running water the fish fare well.

On a hill overlooking town, this small koi pool only has a surface area of 22 m² (266 square feet), but the lovely stone bridge and ideal location enables the pool to support 100 koi, sized 30 to 60 cm, with a water depth of 65 to 80 cm (26 to 32 inches). Rainwater is used to keep the pool clear and fresh.

Surrounded with flowers and covered on one end because the water becomes too green from excessive sun, this 30 m² (about 363 square feet) koi pond looks like a children's swimming pool. Its depth runs from 40 to 100 cm (16 to 40 inches) and it easily supports 80 koi ranging in size from 45 to 55 cm in length.

19

Only 20 m² (about 250 square feet) and very shallow at 50 cm (20 inches) depth, this secluded pool harbors 95 koi ranging in size from 35 to 70 cm. Shallow pools must be protected from the sun and from freezing solid, but they show the koi to their best advantage.

This interesting koi pond runs right under the house. It has a surface area of 60 m² (about 725 square feet) and its depth ranges from 60 to 100 cm (about 24 to 40 inches). The pool supports 200 koi ranging in size from 40 to 80 cm in length.

Natural rocks make ideal stepping stones in this setting which features a small koi pool of 16 m² (about 194 square feet). The water varies in depth from 40 to 100 cm (16 to 40 inches) and supports 40 koi ranging in size from 26 to 60 cm.

In cool seclusion, this koi pond is 40 m² (484 square feet) and ranges in depth from 50 to 100 cm (20 to 40 inches). It contains exactly 50 koi, some of which are 3 feet long.

21

This is a large pool which has a total surface area of 66 m² (about 800 square feet) and a depth of 50 to 165 cm (20 to 65 inches). It contains 80 koi varying in size from 30 to 75 cm. The pool suffers from green water because it gets too much sun and does not have continuous water change nor a filtration system.

By contrast to the pool above, this koi pond is only 35 m² (425 square feet) and a depth of 60 cm (24 inches), yet it contains 80 koi as large as 100 cm (40 inches) and is crystal clear because it is shaded and has running spring water.

A deep rocky pit has been transformed into a beautiful koi pond. The entire surface covers 60 m² (726 square feet) and the water is from 90 to 120 cm (35 to 48 inches) deep. The pond contains 88 koi ranging in size from 20 to 68 cm.

Inside the courtyard of a home, under a roof of grape vines and spreading trees, this charming pond is 66 m² (800 square feet) with a depth of 60 cm (24 inches). There are 400 koi ranging in size from 20 to 60 cm.

Undoubtedly one of the most beautiful koi ponds (note the koi schooling in circles), this Japanese pond measures some 70 m² (about 850 square feet) and has a depth of 160 cm (63 inches). It contains very few koi, only 50, and they range in size from 50 to 75 cm.

At the low end of a large lawn where water had always accumulated, a 33 m² (about 400 square feet) pond at a depth of 100 cm (40 inches) was built. It contains 60 koi ranging in size from 30 to 65 cm.

The owner of this house likes to dangle his feet in the koi pond. Cool running well water keeps the pool clean and fresh. The pond measures 26.4 m² (about 320 square feet), with a depth of about 110 cm (44 inches). It contains 33 large koi, the smallest koi being 50 cm (20 inches) and the largest 75 cm (about 30 inches).

Almost tiny, this 7 m² (85 square feet) pond is very deep at 150 cm (60 inches). Yet it contains 60 koi ranging in size from 15 to 35 cm in length.

A 20 m² pond, 100 cm (40 inches) deep, contains 30 koi ranging in size from 30 to 65 cm. The disadvantages of this design are the koi are too far from the viewer and there is no place to sit and hand-feed the fish.

The board enables a person to feed the koi, while the trees and shrubs keep the sunlight to a minimum, thus enabling the water to remain relatively free of algae. The pool measures 23 m² (278 square feet), has a depth of 60 to 95 cm (24 to 38 inches), and contains 65 koi between 25 and 65 cm in length.

Children and pets are kept out by the fence; the sun is kept from the exposed end by a shade lean-to. The pond is 13.2 m² (about 160 square feet) at a depth of 54 cm (21 inches). There are 96 koi from babies to 60 cm in length.

A truly beautiful and practical pond of 54 m² (about 653 square feet) with a depth of 70 cm (27 inches). There are 90 koi in the pond which measure from 40 to 75 cm in length. The wire protects the fry from the adults.

Beautiful but impractical. The fish are too far away in this 44.6 m² (540 square feet) koi pond which is only 50 cm (20 inches) deep. It contains 80 koi ranging in size from 10 to 50 cm.

A deep pond (130 cm or about 52 inches deep), yet lovely in its simplicity, this 90 m² (1089 square feet) koi pond contains 50 koi ranging in size from 50 to 100 cm.

28

A most impractical koi pond, 30 m² (363 square feet) with a depth of 60 to 110 cm (24 to 43 inches). It contains 60 koi measuring from 15 to 65 cm. The koi are always far from the viewer and hand-feeding them is almost impossible.

Green water is a sign of needed filtration or water change. The ideal koi pond has continually running water. This pond is 30 m² (363 square feet) at a depth of 100 cm (40 inches). It contains 80 koi ranging in size from 50 to 100 cm.

29

This koi pond is built indoors amidst a beautiful rock garden. It measures 15 ㎡ (about 181 square feet) with a depth of 100 cm (40 inches). It contains 30 koi measuring 30 to 60 cm in length.

This intimate pond measures 29 m² (351 square feet) and has a depth of 65 to 100 cm (about 25 to 40 inches). The pool contains 70 koi at a size ranging from 40 to 90 cm.

This is a large natural pond of 600 m² (7300 square feet). It is very deep and contains thousands of koi. The owner invites visitors and sells them feed, thus he has his koi fed and makes a profit too! At one time this was a sand and gravel pit.

Commercial possibilities are to use ponds normally utilized for swimming purposes in the summer, and to stock them with koi kept in a corral. It's a very tricky business, however.

31

## HOW KOI ARE BRED

In Japan, koi are big business. The center of Niigata Prefecture, in gently rolling hill country, contains many small koi farms which produce high quality colored carp that are sold throughout Japan and the rest of the world. No other country has yet been able to produce the same *quality* koi which come from Japan, primarily because they lack the excellent breeding stock and the sales volume necessary to dispose of 100,000,000 koi each year. From these 100,000,000 fish come the handful of champions whose photographs grace these pages.

Each female will lay 200,000 to 400,000 eggs in six hours.

The stone monument at the birthplace of the Koi.

In the early spring of each year special champion fishes are placed into spawning ponds containing a variety of breeding mops. Some breeders use artificial grasses, many use natural plants and dense masses of water hyacinth, but the object is to give the koi fine, bushy plants upon which they deposit their semi-adhesive eggs. A few males and a few females are selected for spawning, having been separated from each other in October of the preceding year. They are placed into small spawning ponds and usually in a day or two the breeder fish deposit their huge spawns. The eggs are then collected with the plants upon which they were deposited and hatched in special hatching ponds. The eggs take about one week to hatch.

The author has taken advantage of this week-long development time and has, on several occasions, imported eggs directly from Japan, packed

Culling starts after six weeks; the fish are one inch long.

During late October, the fry are collected.

The birthplaces of colored carp are scattered in the middle parts of Niigata Prefecture. The center of their origin is considered to have been in about thirty villages formerly called "Yamakoshi Nijyu Songo." Nowadays these villages have been annexed to the cities of Tochiom, Ojiya, and Nagaoka. Yamakoshi Village still remains as the center or origin of koi. The picture is the autumnal scenery of Yamakoshi Village as viewed at Takezawa.

Koi eggs hatching out in a closeup photograph.

Before being liberated in rice paddies, they are again culled.

The culled fry are stored in special ponds to grow.

only in damp moss. Eggs laid in Japan were successfully hatched in warm Florida sunlit pools.

When the koi eggs hatch they are 6 mm in length and are usually transparent. They grow about 1 mm per day and after a month they may be as large as 40 mm (about 25mm=one inch). They begin to color after three weeks of age at which time most of them become orange. As they continue to grow their color continues to change and many cases this color change continues for the whole life of the fish.

Thereafter, for the next few months, the fish go through a continual sorting and culling operation with those fishes which show the most promise separated from the culls. Culls usually are destroyed. By the time the fish reach the midsummer point they are 80 mm (about 3 inches) in length and promising fish can already be selected for growth in outside pools which are rich in mijinko (*Daphnia* or water fleas as some people call them). As soon as the baby koi have ample supplies of this natural food their growth rate is tremendous.

I made several interesting observations during my own spawning experiences. I used rafts of dangling Spanish moss (dried and cured . . . the type used to stuff furniture) in my pools in Flor-

The ponds must be deep enough so they do not freeze completely during the winter.

34

Koi are culled early and the best are kept for future breeding. Only highly colored carp are kept and this photograph shows young (one year olds) which had previously been separated for brood stock.

The slender males chasing heavy, egg-laden females into thickets where their eggs will be deposited. Koi breeding time is the first ten days of May in Japan. In Florida where the author bred millions of koi, the fish bred in late February and early March on rafts of floating dried Spanish moss.

ida. I spawned the koi and removed the rafts to hatch the eggs in concrete vats kept indoors under running water. The koi raised inside did very well, but the koi which resulted from those eggs which fell off the rafts and dropped to the bottom of the pool grew almost twice as fast as those raised indoors! So even eggs which fall into soft silt and mud prove able to hatch. Undoubtedly the natural food found in the outdoor ponds, mainly minute crustaceans and infusorians, are better food than the newly hatched brine shrimp which we fed our tender charges in otherwise sterile concrete vats.

Excess fish are continually culled and stored in concrete vats awaiting sale.

Tochio is a mountainous place rich in the natural beauty of the glittering green leaves of the cedar and the deep red of the fruit of the persimmon. Many professional koi breeders live here.

Koi are reared in ponds like these nestled in the terraced fields of the countryside.

The breeders must be of a good strain in order to get good carp. These carp are selected breeders expected to produce good carp.

Carp Streamers, celebrating the Boy's Festival Day, are raised in almost every house at the beginning of May. Spawning of carp begins about the tenth day of May in Japan.

Male carp violently chase the female in the spawning pond.

38

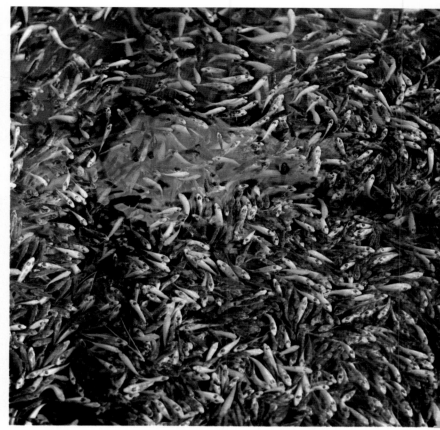

Eggs are transferred to the hatching pond. They will hatch in about one week if the weather is seasonable and warm.

In the last week of June, the first selection of baby carp is conducted. The second one is to be conducted 50 days after the first one, when the koi have grown to be 80 mm. The picture shows the second selection.

Newly hatched fry are 6 mm in length and they are nearly transparent. They grow to 20 mm and their color turns reddish-orange in 20 days. After a month, they should be 40 mm in length.

Selected young carp are released in the rearing pond which is very rich in natural food for carp. Carp rapidly increase their size in this pond.

39

Carp yearlings to be offered for sale are carried from the rearing pond in fields to town where they wait to be shipped.

In late October of the following year, the pond is drained and the fish are hand netted. Only the best koi, called "Tate Goi," are kept in the pond for further growth, the others are sold, usually at auction.

Before the advent of color photography, koi notebooks were available which were merely black outlines of koi printed by wood blocks, page after page. The owner or breeder would fill in the pages with notes on the name of the fish, its price and whatever additional information he felt necessary to record. Additionally, he would color the carp outline by hand to show its color pattern.

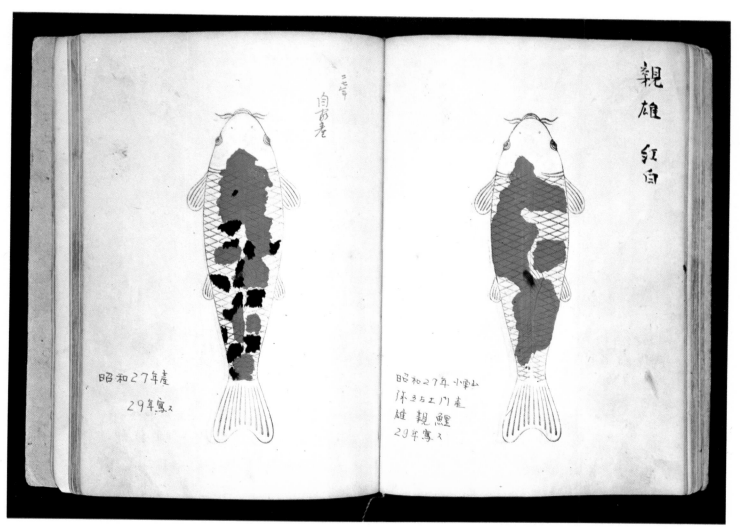

## FISH SALES

In Japan this same procedure is followed until the fish are ready for sale and distribution. Then a unique method of distribution takes place. The best koi are placed into competition where they are categorized into one of five classes or divisions depending upon their size. Within each division are sub-divisions based upon colors and scalation. The winner of each sub-division is easily able to sell his fish for $10,000 or more. As the champions of the sub-division compete against each other for champion of the whole division, the value of the fish increases, until finally the winner of the title BEST FISH IN THE COMPETITION may reach a value of $40,000. Trophies are given to each winner, with the best fish getting a huge trophy, often bigger than the man who wins it!

Those fish which are not entered into competition are sold at auction, in lots of several hundred. Each breeder places his koi into floating wooden cases which are identified by number

Koi are sold at auction by lot number, then loaded onto trucks and rushed to the market as either food or for ornamentation.

only. The floating boxes are opened one at a time in a special viewing gallery several stories high and filled with prospective buyers. As soon as the lid is removed frenzy takes over as bidders keep shouting higher and higher values for the lot. The usual value of these 200 yearling koi runs from about $40 to $60, that is from 10,000 yen to 15,000 yen.

The successful bidders have their huge trucks awaiting their purchases. These trucks are equipped with several 500 gallon wooden vats, each lined with heavy vinyl plastic and filled with very cold, clear water. The fish are dumped into these vats, the vats are sealed, and off rush the trucks racing against time to reach their final destination.

Many breeders hold private sales for their best fish. These breeders prefer not to auction off their fishes; they raise only a few top quality fish and sell them individually. These are usually the sources of the best fish and prices run to unbelievable heights. I witnessed one sale of eleven koi which were sold for $100,000 . . . in cash.

Trophies to be awarded to Winners.

## KOI SHOWS

The fish competitions themselves are interesting. Huge halls are rented and, in some cases, large fields which would normally house sporting events are utilized for displaying the koi to be judged. Wading pools made of blue plastic are filled with 20 cm (about 8 inches) of water and the koi are placed into these pools; ten koi to a pool. Each pool usually contains only one kind of each variety and size of koi. The judges usually select only one koi from each pool as a candidate for a prize. The individual fish selected as a potential winner is eventually placed into an individual aquarium where it is judged more closely for defects which might not be visible from top viewing.

Fish shows are held throughout Japan, in both the large cities and in the small villages. Several koi magazines are published showing excellent color photographs of the winners. The hobby of koi-keeping is not a small, disorganized leisure-time activity. It is a serious, cut-throat business with millions of dollars involved every year.

Putting the carp into the container.

44

The Prize Winner receiving the Trophy.

Show in the rain
held at Beppu City.

Show scene at Taisha City.

Judges evaluating entries.

Thousands of people throng to the koi shows in Japan to view their favorite fish. Wading pools are utilized so people can look down into them.

Sometimes swimming pools become the scenes of koi shows with net baskets to restrain the koi. The advantage of the swimming pool is the filtration system.

The carp has figured in Japanese mythology and painting for hundreds of years as you can see from this painting entitled "Koi in Nishiki-e" done by Utamaro and those on the following pages.

"Cherry Blossoms in March" painted by Toyokuni.

"Early Summer by the Pond" painted by Toyokuni.

48

"Koi in Nishiki-e" by Utamaro (O Nishiki).

## TYPES OF KOI

The Japanese written language is based upon a very unique system. Dictionaries and telephone books are difficult to imagine when you consider that there is no alphabet in Japanese or Chinese. Instead the Japanese rely upon how the Japanese character is written; that is, how many strokes does it take to make a certain character. Those characters which only take one stroke are listed before those characters which take two strokes, etc.

Thus it was quite natural for the Japanese to categorize koi by the numbers, and their number system works something like this. First koi are grouped according to the number of distinct patches of color they possess. Thus there are fishes which have a three-stepped pattern, a four stepped pattern, etc. It is extremely important that the patches of color, the steps, do not in any way connect, for then the value of the patches is reduced. Ideally these patches are indeed steps . . . the kind of steps you might like to find in your Japanese-garden stepping stones allowing you to walk on your fish pond.

After the number of patches comes the number of colors. Solid color fishes, two color fishes, three colors, etc. The combination of steps and colors is always of paramount importance, but such additional characteristics as shape of the patches, depth and intensity of the colors and how distinct the color patches are from the surrounding color are also important.

The final determining factor in koi evaluation is the attractiveness of the color pattern in general. Various categories have been set up to differentiate between color patterns, and as you look through the following pages you will be able to understand some of the color patterns and appreciate the beautiful names given to the various koi varieties.

The final categorization deals with the type of scalation. While most koi are fully scaled, some have scales which are clearly marked and individually isolated colorwise one from the other. Still other types have German scalation where the majority of the body scales are missing. Some koi have such delicate coloration that their scales appear covered with molten gold or silver and if you have never seen one, words alone always fail to prove ample enough to describe this metallic appearance. When I first offered koi for sale in the United States (I stopped selling koi in 1970), I always received the highest price and the most acclaim for Ohgon (gold) metallic-colored koi, even though they are not highly prized in Japan.

The following pages, with very ample captions, show the different kinds of koi much better than any written words can describe. I never fail to daydream everytime I pour through these photographs for almost every fish shown here is a personal friend that I saw swimming in one or another competition in Japan. Is it any wonder that I made more than 25 trips to Japan in the last ten years!

**KOHAKU,** 50 cm in length, weighing 3 kg. The big red patches on the shoulder and the body make up for the defects of the slightly too small red patches on the head and the caudal peduncle. Red patches on this koi are so well distributed as to make it very lovely; its most charming marking is the H-shaped red patch on the body. The snow white provides a good contrast to the deep red patches, and the continued red patches also form good patterns. The edges of the red patches are very distinct. Being favored with a well proportioned body, this fish can boast of its elegance.

**KOHAKU,** 35 cm in length. This photograph shows a typical Kohaku, with red and white coloration. It is a high quality fish. Koi are judged for their appearance from a top view since they are pool fish. This fish is valuable because the divisions between the pure, snow white areas and the deep, dark red are sharply defined and without mismarkings. The color of the dorsal edge in front of the dorsal fin and covering the head almost through to the lip is deep red. The intrusion of white on one side of the dorsal fin ties in with the white dorsal to give the fish a break in the possible monotony of red and enhances by contrast the red area. The red patch on the caudal peduncle is a beautiful saddle mark, making the fish very interesting and balanced, bringing the eye of the viewer to the tail of the fish. It is very, very rare for a Kohaku (red and white koi) to have a red tail.

**KOHAKU,** 42 cm in length. The head patch of red is the shining crown of glory for this very high quality fish. Basically the red "raspberry" head crown is followed by a series of circular red blotches along the entire dorsal edge with just enough white showing to enhance the contrasting red coloration. The body shape of all koi is very important, and this Kohaku has a magnificent physique being heavier and thicker and giving the feeling of strength. Shortcomings in this fish are the poorly defined blotches of red which are more or less outlined with scales of a less intense red coloration. This coloration derives from white scales covering red scales at the edges, thus each red scale is intensely colored and it is just the overlapping which causes the apparent defect.

**KOHAKU,** 48 cm in length, weighing 2.5 kg. The Danmono as a three-step pattern was formerly popular, but it is now becoming a little out of date. This koi is highly regarded for its being a Danmono with the variegated pattern. This pattern is like a 'No Passing' road sign and thus has a nickname of "Oikoshi Kinshi," which in Japanese means "No Passing." The merit of this fish is in the oblique slant of its three-step pattern. The red patches in both the dorsal and the peduncle are well situated.

**KOHAKU,** 50 cm in length, weighing 3 kg. This rather slender koi has three-stepped red patterns. Red patches cover almost the entire body, and the red patches on the head and the shoulder are very large and intense, enhancing the beauty of the fish. The red patches make up for the slenderness of the body. The Kohaku with stepped patterns usually does not have a majestic appearance, but in this koi the first big red patch on the head tends to give it an air of stateliness.

**KOHAKU,** 53 cm in length, weighing 3.5 kg. This is a masterpiece of the Kohaku which has never failed to win when exhibited at a show. The body shape is ideal, and the gorgeous red patches from the head to the peduncle are continual. The elegant shapes of the markings on the head and the shoulder soon draw the viewers' attention, which is very advantageous at the show. The red patches on the body are stately looking. Though the red on the peduncle is situated a little too low, it keeps the patterns in good order. The red is as deep as could be desired in the Kohaku.

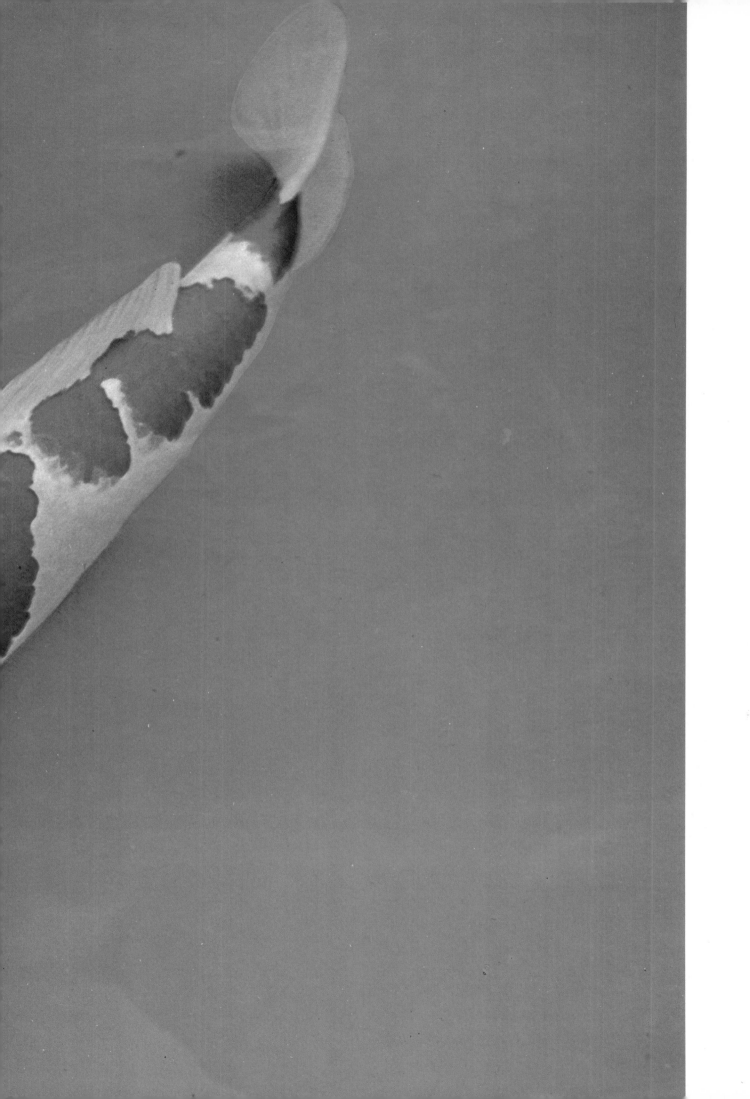

**KOHAKU,** 57 cm in length. This is a very, very high quality fish. It has phenomenal body shape and the very desirable two-step Kohaku pattern. The red is deep and intense and the head patch is remarkably well defined. The first red patch of the two-step pattern is very large and extends from the head to past the middle of the body. The intrusion of white, alternating from one side to the other, makes a very interesting pattern. This first red patch can be envisioned to be the outline of another koi in a swimming motion! Since the red patch does not cover the end of the snout or the eyes it is a perfect red "head." The red patch on the caudal peduncle, sometimes referred to as "Odome" or "Ojime," is likewise well placed and well defined, as well as intensely colored. For a fish as large as this (almost 22 inches in length), it has remarkable body proportions and would probably be judged as a champion fish.

**KOHAKU,** 65 cm in length. As with most pets, people who keep koi in their gardens enjoy keeping them as long as possible. With most fishes, the older they are the larger they are, for fishes continue to grow from the time they are hatched until the time they die. This old female is more than two feet long and has some very interesting color characteristics. Very few koi have a smaller patch of color in the front part of the body as compared to the back, so the slender red patch on the front of this female, compared to her back markings, is desirable and interesting and has earned her the nickname "Yari Kohaku," or "Kohaku with a Spear."

**KOHAKU,** 60 cm in length. As koi get older they, like other animals, usually lose their shape. This very large fish, well over two feet in length, has a very nice physique for its size, and that adds considerably to its value. Colorwise it is not perfect at all. This is a so-called "Three-step Kohaku," there being three distinct areas of red. The first area on the head is by far the superior color characteristic of the fish. It is well defined and doesn't cover the lips, snout or eye. Its outline is sharply defined as well. The second patch of red, lined up, more or less with the dorsal fin, is interesting, though too small. The third mark is small and the caudal peduncle usually bears a heavier mark. The shape of the second and third patches of red form a question mark, which seems to be of interest to some traditionalists.

**TANCHO SANSHOKU,** 45 cm in length. This is a truly magnificent fish. At the time of this writing (1973) this fish was the best Tancho in the world! There were reports (unverified) that the owner of the fish refused $20,000 for it. The red blotch on the head is perfect in size and shape. The heart shape of this red is sharp and clear and well defined. The jet black of the fish is very black and the white is very white, making this an ideal fish in color, form and condition.

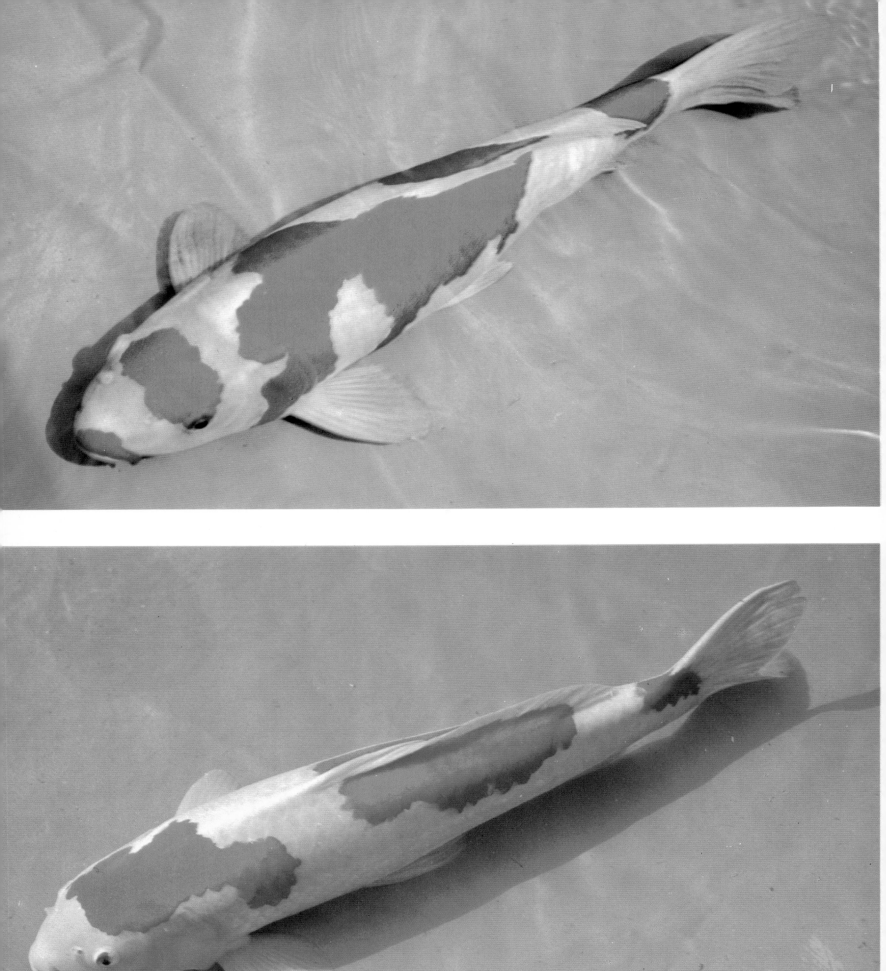

**KOHAKU** (Above), 48 cm in length, weighing 3 kg. This is a Kohaku of three-step pattern with a good body shape. The red patch on the head is the ideal size. The red patch on the shoulder is large and deep, which makes up for the defect in the red patch on the right cheek. The deepness of the red patches also makes up for the defect of the red patch on the left cheek.

**KOHAKU** (Upper left), 46 cm in length, weighing 2.5 kg. This Kohaku has a very well proportioned body. The red, from the lips to the peduncle, is well balanced. The large red patches, from the shoulder to the dorsal area, tend to make this colored carp gorgeous. Though the picture does not reveal them, the red patches on the other side of the fish are four-stepped, and those on the left side are continual. These differences in pattern don't fail at all to balance the koi's entire pattern. The red patch on the peduncle is ideal in its size, shape and position and enhances the fish's beauty.

**KOHAKU** (Lower left), 60 cm in length, weighing 5 kg. A Kohaku having red patches arranged like stepping-stones on its dorsal edge is generally named "Danmono." This is a typical "Sandan Kohaku" three-step pattern), having three big red patches on the dorsal edge. The fish behaves itself as if it were the queen of the pond. The white part is pure white, with no other colors, and the red is also very deep and stands out in strong relief. The big red patch on the shoulder covers up the defect of the thin red tint on the head. Though it is very big, this Kohaku is very graceful in its body shape, being neither fat nor deformed.

**TAISHO SANSHOKU,** 53 cm in length. Typical of the Taisho Sanshoku, with three steps in the red pattern, the first red blotch being well laid out without reaching around the eyes or touching the lips or snout. This is an ideal first step red patch. The black is magnificent, being very sharp and very black, giving the appearance of black patches woven onto a red patchwork quilt. The most spectacular color patches are the last and first red patch, and the black patches on the shoulders. They make interesting markings and are capable of many "ink blot" interpretations. The last red patch is particularly significant in that it doesn't reach the tail. This Odome (last red patch) must be separated from the tail by a white patch in champion koi.

**TAISHO SANSHOKU,** 45 cm in length. This carp has some very fine color characteristics, though it has some undesirable ones as well. The first red patch on the head is sharp and well defined, but runs through the eye and around it. The black is very distinct, however, and the white intrusions make such excellent contrast that the over-all picture makes this a very valuable fish. Most important is the solid, stocky body shape which is so desirable.

**TAISHO SANSHOKU,** 56 cm in length, weighing 5 kg. This fish has a pattern very typical of the Taisho Sanshoku. The red patch on the head, which occupies almost all the part between the eyes, is pure and deep and is to be highly valued, and the solid black on the shoulder is just adjacent to this red patch. This color contrast creates a deep impression among viewers. The snow white scales are fascinating. This koi will always be the first-noticed fish in the pond. It is a true champion.

**DOITSU TAISHO SANSHOKU,** 45 cm in length, weighing 1.5 kg. The red running in a zigzag line on the dorsal edge is very beautiful and makes this koi a gorgeous specimen. The black patch on the shoulder should preferably be a little more solid and congregated, but the other black patches in the lower part of the body are beautifully oriented and make the patterns of the carp well proportioned. The snow white color on both the body and pectoral fins makes this fish as elegant a Taisho Sanshoku as could be desired.

**TAISHO SANSHOKU** (German variety), 35 cm in length. This is the champion of champions in this class and color variety. The very intense color of the red and the brilliance and depth of the black, especially on the shoulders and fins, have made this fish a winner in many competitions.

**AKA SANSHOKU** (German variety), 55 cm in length. This is a very large fish and very beautiful. Red is the predominant color, so the fish is called Aka (which means red) Sanshoku. Outstanding on this specimen is the intensity and magnitude of the red and its sharp definition, punctuated with a very deep black. The black stripes on the pectoral fins and pelvics add grace and harmony and make the red even more contrasting.

**TAISHO SANSHOKU,** 62 cm in length, weighing 10 kg. Though this koi is big the body is well proportioned. The red patch from the rear of the head to the dorsal area is very large and deep and has an imposing appearance. The white part of this fish, unlike that of other big carp, is pure and snow white, which also enhances its beauty. It is generally believed that when a koi grows to a large size its body has a tendency to become deformed, but this big koi is an encouraging exception.

70

**DOITSU TAISHO SANSHOKU,** 50 cm in length, weighing 2 kg. No other Taisho San- shoku has a red patch deeper than that of this koi. The pure and solid red enhances the beauty of the patterns. The red patches make a four-step pattern, and the small red lips (kuchibeni) are very lovely. The red on the peduncle is also very good. The fish has small, clearly colored streaks on the pectoral fins.

**TAISHO SANSHOKU** (German variety), 35 cm in length. This is a truly magnificent specimen with an almost perfect first red step on the head. Japanese gardens and pools almost always have small stepping stones, since the viewer likes to look at the swimming fishes or the blooming flowers as close   to them as possible. This fish has stepping stone markings and has a balanced coloration very rare in koi. It is probably the second best Sanshoku in this book.

**SHIRO BEKKO,** 58 cm in length. This is a perfect classical example of the Shiro Bekko which is a black and white fish. The white must always be as clean as freshly fallen snow, and the black as dark as coal. The very beautiful black stripes on the pectoral fins add to the beauty and symmetry of this well proportioned specimen.

**TAISHO SANSHOKU,** 65 cm in length, weighing 7.5 kg. This majestic koi has an imposing figure, even though its red is not deep. The red lips (kuchibeni) make it a lovely fish. The big red patch from the head to the shoulder enhances its beauty and forms the nucleus of the patterns. The red patches on the body and on the peduncle are as charming as could be desired. This koi can safely be said to be an ideal Taisho Sanshoku.

74

**TAISHO SANSHOKU,**
60 cm in length, weighing 5 kg. This is a typical Taisho Sanshoku with a very elegant appearance. It has a well proportioned body and a snow white color which tends to enhance its beauty. The red patch from the back of the head to the shoulder is very brilliant, which may have made this koi the prize-winner it is. It is gigantic, the size alone well making up for lack of size in the black patches. The distinctive and graceful style of this carp is second to none.

**SHIRO BEKKO,** 65 cm in length. This large fish, about two feet long, has spectacular body form and coloration for such an old fish. Size and age in koi usually run hand-in-hand. The large coal-black patches are uniformly distributed over the body in a very impressive manner. Even the black patch at the base of the pectoral (Motoguro) is advantageous and this is typical of fishes which are valued by Japanese koi fanciers.

**HI SHOWA,** 42 cm in length. This is a very beautiful fish. It has good form and excellent coloration combining a deepness of black with contrasting red. The pectorals are very beautiful, black at the base and white on the extremes. The head marking of red with a trailing irregular black streak is very unusual.

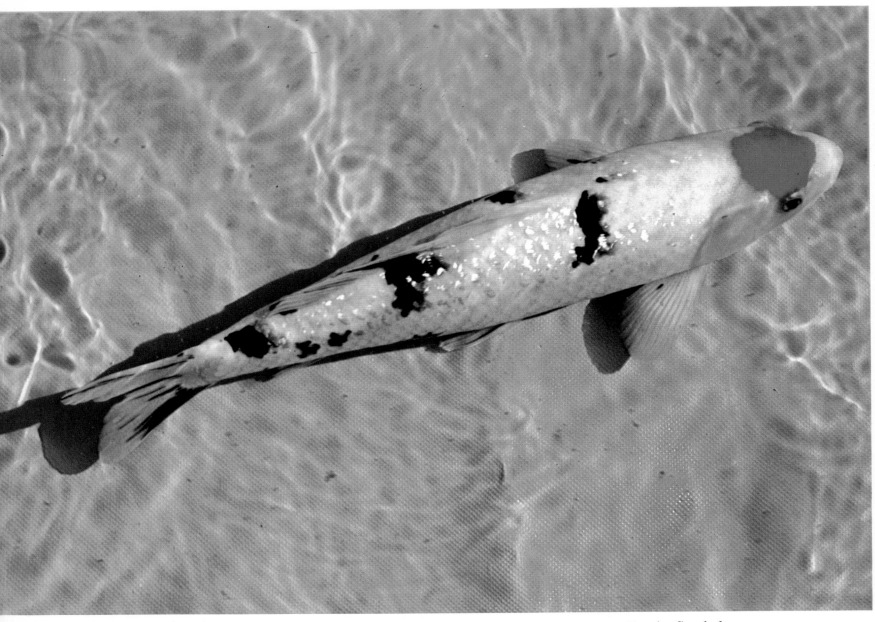

**TANCHO SANSHOKU GINRIN,** 36 cm in length, weighing 1 kg. This is a very elegant Tancho Sanshoku. The red patch on the head is properly big and deep enough. The presence of only a few black patches may be a defect, but the black patches themselves are very solid and cover up the sameness of the pattern. The Ginrin, which runs along the dorsal edge, enhances the beauty of this koi. The Ginrin lustrous scales are large in number and well scattered along the proper part of the body, making this carp an ideal Ginrin.

**SHOWA SANSHOKU** (right), 55 cm in length, weighing 3.5 kg. This koi looks very virile, for it has the typical patterns of the Showa Sanshoku. The body is primarily covered with a solid black patch; the red is very deep. The contrast between the solid black and deep red attracts the attention of viewers. The small white patch on the rear part of the left side of the body is snow white and enhances the fish's beauty. Small red speckles in the white part give a very lovely appearance to the carp. Its pectoral fins are the desirable solid black. The head is a little too large, but this adds manliness to the carp.

**SHOWA SANSHOKU,** 25 cm in length. Typical of the Showa is the black patch on the snout of the fish. This is still a young fish, about two years old, and if its color becomes enhanced, it will certainly be a difficult fish to beat in competition in a few years. The large black patch covering the head and shoulders is nicely balanced by the deep red patch which surrounds most of it. The striking white patch leading up to the dorsal fin on one side of the fish is very attractive and interesting and it breaks the continuity of the black and red alternations.

**SHOWA SANSHOKU,** 55 cm in length. It is rare to find a large fish with such a fine body. To add to this character such magnificent and interesting coloration has to result in a fish of great charm and beauty . . . to say nothing of value. You must study the color patterns on the back of this koi to appreciate its beauty. The symmetry of the black patch actually mimics an "ink blot" which has been trapped between two pieces of paper and then spread out. Truly a magnificent fish!

**SHOWA SANSHOKU,** 36 cm in length, weighing 1 kg. This koi has the typical Showa Sanshoku pattern. As the red is distributed over the entire body, it may well be called 'Hi Showa.' The red is deep, and the solid black is well combined with the big red patches on the head. This koi is truly worthy of being called "Swimming Treasure."

**SHOWA SANSHOKU,** 42 cm in length, weighing 2 kg. This is an ideal Showa Sanshoku in its proportion of black, red and white coloration. These colors are ideally distributed. The intensity of each color is very deep. The very small white part in the middle of the right side of the body is pure white and makes a very good contrast to the other colors. The defect of the separated black patch on the head part is compensated for by the big solid black patch on the shoulder. The very deep red patch from the forehead to the shoulder makes this koi gorgeous. The red patch on the peduncle is very distinctive and makes itself a part of the well proportioned pattern of this beautiful koi.

**SHIRO UTSURI,** 62 cm in length. A very colorful and well formed specimen for such a large fish. The white areas are free of stains and the symmetry of the black areas is highly commendable. An interesting black patch on the head is nicely balanced by the black patches on each side of the body in a well balanced pattern. The distinct black and white areas make this an outstanding koi.

**SHIRO UTSURI** (German variety), 40 cm in length. This is a very prime example of scaleless white areas and velvet black areas in a very interesting pattern. The stark contrast between black and white, the two colors which contrast maximally, makes this fish extremely noteworthy.

**SHOWA SANSHOKU,** 55 cm in length, weighing 4 kg. This is a brilliant female Showa. The red patch on the head makes a deep impression on the observer. The black patches on the snout and on the head part are those of the typical Kobayashi Showa, and the red and black patches on the body make this koi one of the best Showa. There is a strain of the Showa Sanshoku called "Hi Showa" in which the red predominates. But the Menkaburi ("wearing a red mask") is to be avoided. This koi has white patches on the cheek and on the sides of the body. These white patches are pure white which tends to enhance the beauty of this fish.

86

**SHOWA SANSHOKU,** 42 cm in length, weighing 2 kg. The pattern on the head is that of a typical Showa Sanshoku. The red patches from the head to the shoulder are large and so deep that the solid black in contact with these red patches looks especially conspicuous. This is a very masculine Showa. The body is rather of a male type, and the pectoral fins, which are black at the base, are lovely. The pattern in the rear part of the body is rather poor, which may be considered a defect of this koi, but the solid black on the shoulder makes up for this defect, making this fish a typical Showa.

**HI-UTSURI,** 50 cm in length. This is almost a champion quality Hi-utsuri because of the bulky, compact shape of the fish. The wide, broad shape of the pectoral fins and the well placed very black patches on the fins and on the body are noteworthy. The black markings on the head divide the brilliant, deep red into two parts which the Japanese call "Menware." On the caudal end of the fish the black patches are well shaped and the red caudal peduncle is intensely colored without black markings. Hi-utsuri koi must be lustrous and this koi has a highly glazed appearance not especially detailed in this photograph.

**SHIRO KAGE UTSURI,** 50 cm in length. The depth of the coal black markings and the interesting manner in which the black is distributed over the body make this a prime example of the black and white koi. The black head markings make a mask which divides the head region into two very distinct areas. The mask continues in a connecting manner throughout the body like a delicate black net enhancing the white areas and making the koi extremely attractive. The pectorals are also nicely marked.

**SHOWA SANSHOKU,**
62 cm in length, weighing
5 kg. The pure red of this
Showa is predominant.
The black streaks begin
at the snout and they
symmetrically combine
with the red patches. The
black streaks are very
solid, which well proclaim
the fish as one of the
Showa Sanshoku. As it
has adequate white parts
and is a gigantic female,
it overwhelms other koi
and draws the attention
of the fanciers.

**KAGE HI-UTSURI,**
48 cm in length, weighing 2 kg. The author had assumed that the name "Kage Utsuri" was given to bad specimens of Utsurimono with poor back colors by dealers who want to sell such koi at high prices. But this fish made me abandon such a notion. It has the characteristics of the Utsurimono and has solid black. The big solid black on the shoulder gives a good accent to the koi. The deeper red patch is reticulated with black and gives a queer appearance to the fish compared with other kinds of koi. This is one of the best specimens of the Utsurimono.

**SHUSUI,** 70 cm in length. This very large fish, about 28 inches long, is the champion Shusui of the world (1973) because of its magnificent body shape and interesting color pattern. The large scales are unbelievably uniform as they lay along the dorsal edge. The silvery lustre of the edges of these dorsal scales (which show as white in the photograph) accentuates this uniform row of scales and is extremely rare in such a large fish. Koi lose their scale lustre as they get older and larger. Parallel to this row of scales are bright red bands running almost perfectly homologous so the fish is colored almost bilaterally symmetrically, again a very rare color pattern for koi. The author has never seen a better example of a Shusui.

**KOHAKU** (Sarasa) are red and white koi. This is the oldest race of Japanese multi-colored carp and is still one of the world's favorites, winning many competitions. Modern Kohaku, such as that shown above, are believed to have descended from stock produced by Kunizo Hiroi in 1889. They were grown in Higashiyama Village, Niigata Prefecture, Japan.

**HI-UTSURI,** 60 cm in length, weighing 7 kg. No carp is more astoundingly beautiful than this. The typical Utsurimono patterns are deeply impressive. The deep red is second to none as the deep red of an Utsurimono. The solid black is also proportionally well situated. Good Hi-utsuri are rare and the usual Hi-utsuri have defective red patches which are usually speckled with small black dots, but this koi has very few speckles, which may be why it looks so smart.

94

**HI-UTSURI**, 70 cm in length, weighing 7 kg. No larger specimen can be more beautiful in its body proportion than this. The solid black which is one of the characteristics of the Utsurimono is beautifully situated and enhances the beauty of the fish. The red patch on the Hi-utsuri is likely to be stained with small black speckles, but this koi has a pure red patch with no black speckles.

The red is not so deep, but this fact rather tends to make this carp elegant.

It has beautiful streak patterns in the pectoral fins. The fish is such a masterpiece that it soon attracts viewers' attention in the pond and teaches us that one of the principles of koi evaluation is to take the body proportion into consideration first.

**NIDAN KOHAKU,** the two-stepped Kohaku, is characterized by two distinct red areas. In desirable specimens the front patch must be relatively large but must not cover the entire head and must never reach the tip of the snout nor the lips. The rear red patch should be well balanced in size when compared to the front red patch, and should be well formed. This is an ideal specimen of the Nidan Kohaku.

**SANDAN KOHAKU,** the three-stepped Kohaku, must have three distinct patches of red, each unconnected to the others. This variety is also known as the Sandan Moyo (Three-step Pattern) and Sandan Hi (Three-step Scarlet). This fish is far from a prized specimen because the red patch touches the eyes and the rear red patch touches the tail. However the excellent intensity of color, the large size of the three red patches and the distinctness of the patch on the head make this a valuable fish nevertheless.

**HI-UTSURI,** 60 cm in length, weighing 5 kg. The red of this carp is between that of the Ki-utsuri and that of a typical Hi-utsuri. The red of the Hi-utsuri is likely to be stained with black speckles, and this tendency deforms the fish. But the black patches of this koi are well congregated and make it look elegant; the specimen's merit is in the oblique black patch from the shoulder to head. The streaked patterns of the Hi-utsuri are seen even in the pectoral fins, which enhance the fish's beauty.

**KOHAKU** (red and white). The main color is white with red patches on the dorsal edge. This is one of the most common types of Japanese colored carp. The Kohaku which were kept in the days of Bunka and Bunsei (1804-1830) had a simple pattern in which the red patch appeared either only on the head or covered almost the entire body except the ventral area which was white.

**YONDAN KOHAKU,** the four-stepped Kohaku, has four distinct, unconnected red patches. The first step on this fish is the red lip which is known as "Kuchibeni" in Japanese. Unfortunately on the specimen shown above the red patch on the lip is too large, but this is partially compensated for by the beautiful last step which is the red patch so beautifully separated from the tail by a clear white patch. The second and third steps are two really beautiful, distinct, separated red patches, nicely balanced on the head and straddling the dorsal origin. Overall the color pattern is very pleasing.

**BENI GOI,** the Aka Muji pure red koi shown above, looks very much like a goldfish. A good specimen must be completely red, including all fins and the entire body including the belly. The fish is judged by the intensity and depth of the red coloration.

**KUCHIBENI KOHAKU,** the red-lip Kohaku. The adjective "Kuchibeni" is an often used Japanese word which is frequently applied to many color varieties of koi. Thus, if a Taisho Sanshoku has red lips it can be called a "Kuchibeni Taisho Sanshoku." Normally the fish shown here would be called a Three-stepped Kohaku, but since the first patch (step) is on the lips, it is called a "Kuchibeni Kohaku." An obvious defect in this specimen is the white patches intruding into the red above and behind the eye of the fish, but this is offset by the red lip patch.

**NIDAN KOHAKU** (two-step pattern). This is a Kohaku whose red patches along the dorsal edge are divided into two divisions.

**SANDAN KOHAKU** (three-step pattern). This is a Kohaku whose red patches along the dorsal part are divided into three divisions.

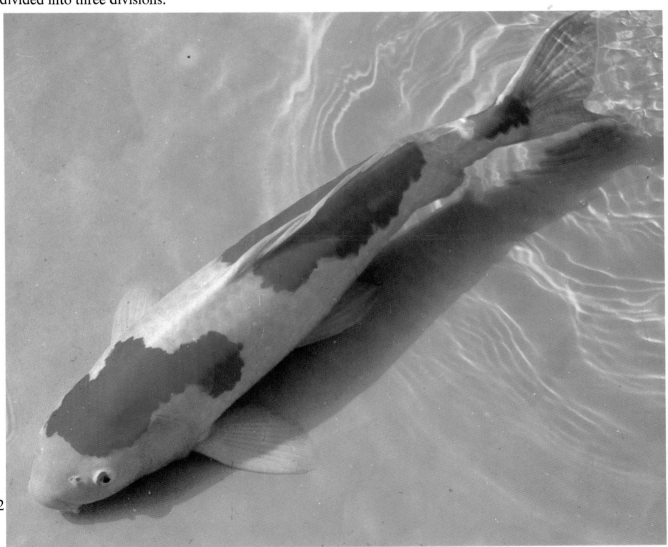

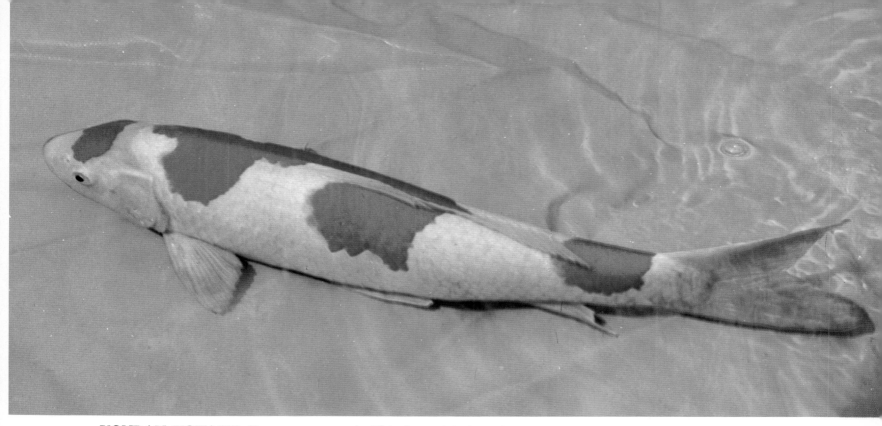

**YONDAN KOHAKU** (four-step pattern). This is a Kohaku whose red patches along the dorsal part are divided into four divisions.

**INAZUMA KOHAKU** (red in zig-zag pattern). This is a Kohaku whose red pattern runs in a zig-zag line on the dorsal edge of the body. The typical Inazuma Kohaku owned by Shoichi Osaki received the Prime Minister's Prize at the Second National Show of the Colored Carp. Since then this type of the Kohaku has become very popular.

**INAZUMA KOHAKU,** the zig-zag Kohaku, is characterized by the zig-zag pattern of the red coloration. The defect in the specimen shown in this photograph is that the red over the head does not extend far enough onto the gill covers. The red zig-zag patch is so contrasting, broad and colorful, however, that it more than offsets the operculum coloration defect.

**GOTENSAKURA KOHAKU,** the palace cherry blossom Kohaku, is a very attractive variety of koi. When small red patches are scattered about the body of the koi against a white background as shown in this specimen, the fish is called "Gotensakura." In this variety each scale must be so graduated in color that it appears they are non-overlapping and separate from each other. A defect of this specimen is that the red coloration on the gill cover extends too far.

**MENKABURI KOHAKU** (Above). This is a Kohaku whose red marking on the head covers almost the entire head. The Menkaburi Kohaku was often seen in early days but it is now disliked if the red entirely covers the head part even when other red patches are properly situated.

**KUCHIBENI KOHAKU** (Red Lips) (Lower). This is a Kohaku with red markings on the mouth part. This characteristic makes the carp very lovely and so the Kuchibeni is highly admired.

**GOTENSAKURA KOHAKU** (palace cherry blossom). This is a Kohaku whose red scales have so many erythrophores that they seem to have swollen up as if they were a bunch of grapes. It is one of the early Kohaku which was kept in the Meiji Period (1868-1912). The Gotensakura Kohaku owned by Shoichi Osaki may well be said to be the best Gotensakura Kohaku that has ever appeared.

**KANOKO KOHAKU,** the fawn Kohaku, derives its name from the Japanese word "Kanoko," which means a year-old fawn with its typical white spots on a tan background. Koi which have red spots are named after the fawn and are highly prized and very rare. An ultimate koi, and one never seen to date (1973), is a completely dappled koi. Pink-eyed albino koi are those most often found with a dappled color pattern. The specimen shown above is defective because of the poor red patch on the head.

**TANCHO KOHAKU,** usually just called "Tancho," is named after a Japanese crane which also has a red patch on the head. The ideal Tancho has a snow white body and a large red patch on the head; the larger the patch and the whiter the body, the better the specimen. Further breakdowns of this category depend upon the shape of the red patch on the head. Those Tancho which have a heart-shaped red patch are known as Hato Tancho (heart-shaped Tancho); there are also Kakutan Tancho (square-shaped Tancho) and, as is the case with the fish illustrated here, Hinomaru Tancho (round-shaped after the Japanese National Rising Sun Flag, Tancho.)

**KANOKO KOHAKU** (fawn). This is a Kohaku whose red patches are not so much congregated but finely variegated as markings on young deer. This is seen in rather old style Kohaku.

**KINSAKURA KOHAKU** (golden cherry blossom) (Right). This is a Gotensakura Kohaku whose red scales are reticulated with a golden tint. This is a very splendid carp.

110

**TANCHO KOHAKU** (Above). This is a Kohaku whose red marking is only on the head. The red marking is usually a round one but sometimes it is heart-shaped and the carp with this heart-shaped red marking is called "Heart Tancho." Tancho means the crane (*Grus japonensis*) which is a white bird with a red patch on the head.

**MENKABURI KOHAKU,** the masked Kohaku, is a beautiful variety which has its entire head covered with red. This relatively new variety is not appreciated by the Japanese because they feel the fish to be too gaudily decorated and not aristocratic in appearance. This specimen has a horrible defect in that the red coloration which covers the head runs onto the pectoral fins. The Japanese disparagingly call this defect "Aka Te," which means "red hands," a name applicable to dishwashers. The body shape of this fish is also unbecoming.

**SHIRO MUJI,** the plain white koi with black eyes, is not an albino. The coloration derives from guanophores, the color cells found in the scales, which are spread completely over the body. The full beauty of this fish can only be appreciated when the fish is large and the scales turn a lemon yellow color. When the scales of this variety are metallic in appearance, the fish is known as "Ginrin."

**TAISHO SANSHOKU** (Taisho tri-color). Its main color is white and it is beautifully patterned with red and black patches. The black must be velvety black and the red must also be very deep. The pectoral fins are required to be beautifully streaked. Heitaro Sato is reputed to have found the original Sanshoku amongst fry of the Kohaku in 1915. Eizaburo Hoshino is said to have improved the Sanshoku, using this original Sanshoku, in 1917.

**TANCHO SANSHOKU** (red-headed tri-color). This is a Taisho Sanshoku whose red marking is only on the head.

**TAISHO SANSHOKU** is a color pattern with many varieties. Basically Taisho Sanshoku have three colors, white, red and black. Especially sought after are specimens which have black streaks on their pectoral fins. This variety was first developed by Eizburo Hoshino who bred koi in Takezawa Village in Niigata Prefecture, Japan. He produced this color variety in 1917. On this specimen the red patches are excellent but the black patches are too small. The black streaks in one pectoral fin are excellent; in the other they are mediocre.

**TANCHO SANSHOKU** is a red-headed three colored koi, but the red can exist only as a head patch as shown here. This specimen is defective because the eyes also have red rims and this is a very serious defect.

**AKA MUJI** (plain red) (Above). It is sometimes called 'Hi-goi.' This is one of the earliest colored carp. The color of the body is entirely red and no other colors nor maskings should be seen.

**SHIRO MUJI** (plain white) (Right upper). It has little or no xanthophores, erythrophores nor melanophores on the body. Its only chromatophores are guanaphores. So the carp is plain white. There are two strains on the Shiro Muji: black eyes and pink eyes (albino).

**BENI GOI** (Right lower). This is an Aka Muji whose red has become so much deeper.

**AKA HAJIRO.** This is an Aka Muji with white pectoral fins.

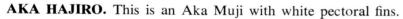

118

119

**AKA SANSHOKU,** the red Sanshoku, must have its body almost completely covered in red, with orderly, well-placed black patches. The difference between this color variety and the Aka Bekko is that the Aka Bekko does not have any white. A really perfect specimen would be solid red completely and overlaid with deep, coal black patches.

**SHIRO BEKKO,** the white tortoiseshell koi, derives its name from Shiro = white and Bekko = tortoiseshell. This color variety is predominantly snow white with coal black patches of black arranged in an orderly manner along the dorsal edge. In really exceptional specimens the head should have one black patch isolated from the other black patches. Unfortunately, this specimen does not show that characteristic. Further shortcomings of this fish are the small black dapples which mismark the area in front of the large black patch which runs from the head to the shoulders.

**SHIRO BEKKO** (white tortoise shell) (Above). The main color is white with black patches neatly dotted on the dorsal edge of the carp. "Bekko" means tortoise-shell whose pattern is like that of this carp. The best specimens must have solid white and must be neatly dotted with black patches along the dorsal part. A round black patch on the head is desirable for the Shiro Bekko.

**AKA BEKKO** (red tortoise shell) (Left). The main color is red and black patches are dotted on the dorsal edge of the body. It is rather gaudy in its color combination.

**AKA SANSHOKU** (red tri-color) (Above). This is a Taisho Sanshoku whose red pattern dominates the three colors. The red runs from the head to the dorsal in which black markings are scattered. The small white portion distinguishes this from the Aka Bekko.

**KI BEKKO.** The main color is yellow and black patches are scattered as in other Bekko strains.

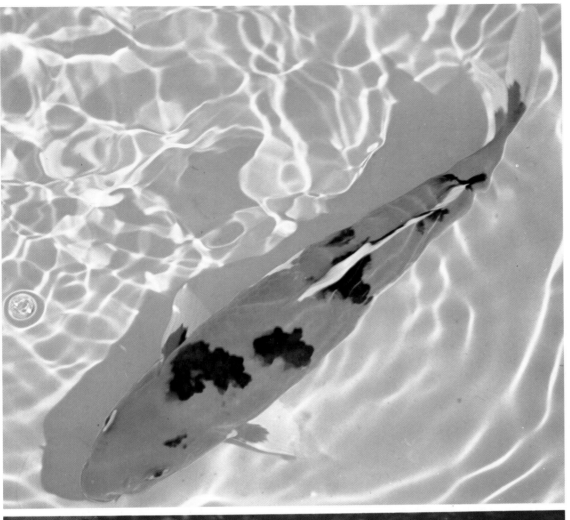

**AKA BEKKO,** the red tortoiseshell, is a color variety which is predominantly deep red and decorated with black patches arranged in an orderly manner along the dorsal edge. This is a rare color variety and the specimen shown is a good one.

**KI BEKKO,** the yellow tortoiseshell, is not a common color variety at all. Basically the fish is golden yellow, almost light orange, with scattered and distinct patches of coal black. The Hikari Mono color variety of the Ki Bekko is known as the "Tora Ohgon" or golden tiger. This is a poor specimen since the black patches are not a deep coal black and are not distinct and contrasted.

**SHOWA SANSHOKU** is a three-color koi whose basic color is black, with additional smatterings of red and white. Showa Sanshoku must have a black patch somewhere on the head in front of the insertion of the pectoral fins; Taisho Sanshoku, by contrast, do not have this black head patch. In good quality Showa Sanshoku, the black area should cover the entire dorsal girdle reaching the abdomen, while the pectoral fins have the Motoguro pattern which is a black patch at the base of the fin which radiates outward. This color variety was perfected and bred by Jyukichi Hoshino of Takezawa Village, Niigata Prefecture, Japan in 1927.

**HI SHOWA** (red Showa tri-color) (Above). This is a Showa Sanshoku whose red extends almost entirely on the body.

**SHOWA SANSHOKU** (Showa tri-color). This carp is basically black with red and white patches. The black patch of the Taisho Sanshoku is only on the dorsal area; that of the Showa Sanshoku extends to the ventral area. The bases of pectoral fins are required to be black. This Koi may have been produced from the crossing of the Ki Utsuri and the Kohaku by Shigekichi Hoshino in 1927. This is rather a rare carp to be obtained and the prices for good specimens are often very high. It is now a very popular carp among koi fanciers. "Showa" designates (in Japan) the present era of Emperor Showa, 1926 to date.

**KINDAI SHOWA** (Modern Showa tri-color) is a Showa Sanshoku whose white area is more extensive on the body. This carp resembles the Taisho Sanshoku. The shapes of the black patches are not like those of the Taisho Sanshoku, however, but like those of the Showa Sanshoku.

**KINDAI SHOWA,** a modern Showa, is a color variety of the Showa Sanshoku which has a preponderance of white. At first glance this fish might easily be confused with the Taisho Sanshoku. But this fish has a black head spot, not a red one, and the color pattern of the pectorals is quite different.

**HI SHOWA,** the red Showa, is a color variety of the Showa Sanshoku which features numerous large patches of red distributed fairly uniformly over the entire body. The specimen shown here is almost perfect, but the caudal peduncle is lacking in a balancing red patch. The Motoguro (black pectoral patch) and head patches are exceptionally fine.

**TANCHO SHOWA** (red crested Showa) (Upper). This is a Showa Sanshoku whose red patch is confined only to the head.

**KAGE SHOWA** (Lower). This is a Showa Sanshoku whose black patches fade off to a shadow. It is a carp with very quiet patterns.

130

## Shiro Utsuri (White Reflection)

The basic color is solid black and there are white patches on the body. This derives from the Ma Goi (Wild carp). The bases of pectoral fins are required to be black.

**AI SHOWA.** This is a Showa Sanshoku whose patches contain indigo speckles.

**TANCHO SHOWA** is a Showa Sanshoku which has the characteristic red patch on the head . . . and only on the head. This is a very rare color variety of Showa Sanshoku, and the best specimens have very well shaped, circular, deep velvet red head patches. The body pattern must also be deep coal black and interestingly distributed. This specimen has a magnificent head patch, but the black patches along the sides and back of the fish are not black enough.

**KAGE SHOWA,** the silhouetted Showa, is a color variety within the Showa Sanshoku which is characterized by the white and red scales being covered by a layer of transparent gray scales giving the fish a dirty appearance. If the overall appearance of this fish is like a net wherein the gray lies inside the scale and the red and white edges of the scales show in great contrast, then that characteristic is the most important. This specimen has an excellent body shape, and the black head patch is dark and interestingly shaped.

**BOKE SHOWA**

**HI-UTSURI**

**BOKE SHOWA** (Upper left). This is a Showa Sanshoku whose black patches have faded into reticular patterns or splashed patterns.

**HI-UTSURI** (red reflection) (Lower left) is a Ki Utsuri whose yellow patches have become deeper and turned red. This is a two-tone carp of solid black and red. Big specimens of this carp make a magnificent impression. The specimen with deep red patches is highly valued.

**KAGE-UTSURI** (silhouetted) (Upper right) is a Shiro Utsuri whose white patches are reticulated and stained with black. Dr. Yoshiichi Matsui says that the melanophores are liable to appear on the dorsal area of the carp, and this tendency is called "Se Guro Sei" which means "black dorsal area." The Kage Utsuri may safely be said to be the Shiro-Utsuri with melanophores in the white patches on the dorsal area.

**KI-UTSURI** (yellow reflection) (Right lower) is one of the early colored carp. In the early days of the Meiji era, there was a good specimen of this carp, which was named "Kuro Ki Madara" (black mottled with yellow). As the name indicates, this is a black carp with yellow patches.

**KAGE-UTSURI**

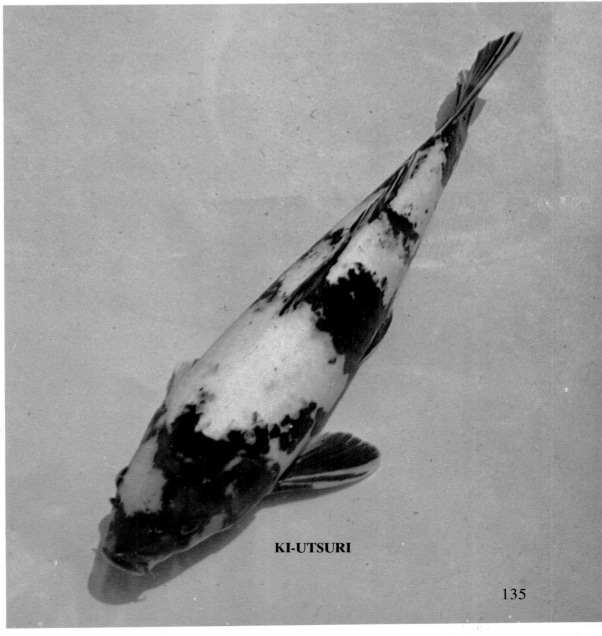

**KI-UTSURI**

135

**AI SHOWA** is a color variety of Showa Sanshoku which features red scales tinged with blue. Blue is a "dream" color for many fish fanciers, not only koi and goldfish fanciers. There are very few koi as magnificent in color and body shape as the one shown here. The red patches on the head, so deeply colored and so distinct and well shaped, plus the very black patches, make this a champion-quality fish.

**BOKE SHOWA** is a color variety of Showa Sanshoku characterized by indistinct black patches which form a mottled or net-like veil over the major part of the koi's body. This fish may be classified as a Showa even though it has no intense black patches, as long as it has a definite net-like appearance created by contrasting scale edges. The intensity and pattern of the red and the beautiful net-like pattern of the scales make this a very high quality fish.

**SHUSUI** (autumn sky) is a mirror carp whose dorsal side is blue or light blue and whose ventral side is red. In the Meiji Period (1868-1912), Kichigoro Akiyama, a famous breeder of carp and goldfish, produced this new strain of the colored carp as a hybrid of a female German carp and a male Asagi. This new one was blue on the dorsal side with scales of a mirror carp.

**HANA SHUSUI** (Above). This is a Shusui having beautiful red patterns on the lips, the cheeks and the ventral area.

**HI SHUSUI** (Below) is a Hana Shusui whose red parts extend to the entire body.

139

**HI-UTSURI** are koi which have a basic black body upon which red patches are interestingly and artistically dispersed. A very sharp contrast and distinct separation between red and black is essential; many inferior specimens have red patches which are blemished with black specks. A velvet covering is a desirable objective in this color variety, and the specimen shown is quite beautiful in this regard. The main defect of this fish is the pectoral fins which are almost all black instead of having the desirable Motoguro pattern which is black at the base with radiating black rays toward the tips of the fins.

**SHIRO-UTSURI,** the white reflection koi, is basically a black fish with white markings. The pectoral fins must be Motoguro, which is black at the base with radiations extending from the black base blotch. This variety was originated by Kazuo Minemura at his home in Mushigame City, Niigata Prefecture, Japan in 1925. The specimen shown here is a good one since the black pattern is deep and interesting, sharply contrasted against white.

**SHOWA SHUSUI** has two-fold characteristics of both the Showa Sanshoku and the Shusui. It is highly prized as a rare carp.

**SANSHOKU SHUSUI.** This is a carp having two-fold characteristics of both the Taisho Sanshoku and the Shusui.

142

**KAWARI SHUSUI** (Shusui variety) (Above). This is a variation of the Shusui which is two-tone with dark gray and golden brown. Very rare.

**GOSHIKI SHUSUI** (Lower). This is thought to have been produced as a result of the crossing of the Goshiki and the Shusui. The main color is blue; waving black patterns are seen on the ventral side and the red hue is seen on the base of the pectoral fins and in the ventral area.

143

**SHIRO KAGE UTSURI,** the silhouetted white reflection koi, is a color variety of the Shiro-utsuri with indistinct white patches which have the characteristic light gray or blue scale pigmentation which lies inside the perimeter of the white scales giving them a net-like appearance. The more defined the net, the more valuable the specimen. The pectoral fins must be Motoguro. This specimen is not nicely patterned but the net-like pattern is beautiful.

**KI-UTSURI,** or yellow reflection, is a black koi with yellow patches. This is a very old color variety and was known as far back as the Meiji period when it was called "Kuro ki Madara." The modern Ki-utsuri probably descended from stock produced by Eizburo Hoshino in 1920, but they are very rare, especially those specimens with a yellow or yellow-orange coloration. This is a very poor specimen because the black coloration is sub-standard.

**HI KAGE UTSURI,** the silhouetted red reflection koi, is a Hi-utsuri variety which has red scales covered by a blue or gray net. This is a truly great specimen because of the magnificent body shape, the intense, contrasting color patches and the very clear net-like effect on the red scales.

**ASAGI** (pale or light blue). The dorsal half of the body is grayish blue with reticulated scales. It has red patches on the cheeks and the ventral edge. As each scale is surrounded by whitish color, the body looks somewhat obscure. Asagi are classified as the Konjo Asagi (deep blue), the Narumi Asagi (blue), the Taki Asagi (Asagi with one long white streak as if it were a waterfall) and the Akebi Asagi (palest blue).

**BUDO SANSHOKU.** Masatomo Kataoka says that this is rarely obtained from the fry of the Kohaku or the Goshiki. It has an intermediate tint of the Aigoromo and the Sumigoromo. It may be said to be a variegated carp of reddish purple and white.

**GOSHIKI** (five colors). The reticulated scales of the Asagi are seen like small black speckles in this carp as each scale has a broad edge of white. This is thought to be a hybrid of the Asagi and the Aka Bekko. The body has a somewhat purplish hue with small red speckles and black flecks. It has rather a quiet pattern. The deeper the red, the better.

147

**SHUSUI,** the autumn ski koi, is a variety of the Asagi Shusui color group. This color variety was produced by Kichigoro Akiyama during the late Meiji period by crossing Asagi with German Mirror Carp. The dorsal areas are noted for their Prussian blue color, and a very desirable characteristic is intense, deep velvet red markings on the gill covers, pectoral fins and abdomen. The specimen shown here is a typical Shusui with the large German-type scales beautifully arranged along the dorsal edge, glittering with a metallic lustre. This fish has several defects in that the head should be unmarked and completely white, while the gill covers should have more red pigmentation.

**HI-SHUSUI,** the red autumn sky, is a Shusui whose color is predominantly red and whose Prussian blue patches are reduced. This specimen has a good head because it is almost pure white without any red pigmentation, and the almost perfect line of German scales along the dorsal edge is uniform, metallic and well formed. If the scales were perfect, the fish would be much more valuable as the German scales near the end of the dorsal are indistinct.

**ASAGI SAN-SHOKU.** This is a variation of the Asagi. It has vague Asagi-type patterns on the dorsal area with deep red patterns on its cheeks; creamy white patterns on the ventral area.

**BUNKA SAN-SHOKU** (Fuji koi) was produced as a result of mating the Taisho Sanshoku with the Shusui. The edges of the pectoral fins have glittering tints. The Fuji koi is a variation of the Bunka Sanshoku with its head and back glittering.

**HAGOROMO** (robe of feathers). This is one of the Asagi strains and has many similar points to the Aigoromo (blue mantle). Its main color is dark grayish blue. It has red on the cheeks and the pectoral fins.

150

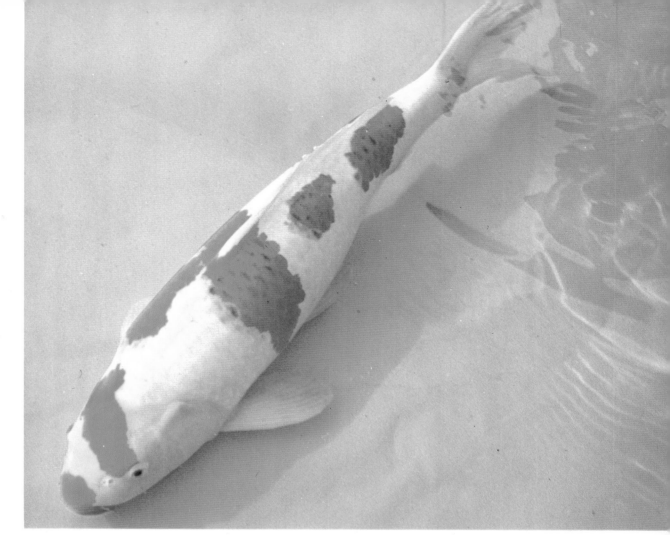

**AIGOROMO** (blue mantle). This results from a crossing of the Kohaku and the Asagi. The red patches of the Kohaku are inlayed with small blue speckles. Dr. Matsui says that this is a Kohaku with a black dorsal area.

**SUMIGOROMO.** This is a crossing of the Kohaku and the Asagi. The red patches contain small black speckles.

151

**HANA SHUSUI** differ from ordinary Shusui by the fact that their red pigmentation is so high on the body and is arranged in a wavy or spotted pattern. This color variety of Shusui must have deep red patches with very light Prussian blue scales. The head patch must be perfectly colored. This fish is defective because the red areas of the body have black intrusions.

**SHOWA SHUSUI,** the autumn sky Showa, is a hybrid which resulted from a cross between the Showa San-shoku and the Shusui and incorporates features of both color varieties. The major difference between the Showa Shusui and the Doitsu (German) Showa is that the Showa Shusui has a blue cast to the dorsal edge while the German doesn't. The derivation of the Japanese word "Doitsu" is simple. "Doitsu" is pronounced "doy-ts" with the final "u" silent. That's what the Germans call themselves . . . deutsch. The specimen shown here has the nice white head which characterizes the Shusui, while the black patches derive from the Showa heritage.

**OHGON** (gold). This is a magnificent golden carp with reticulated scales. The original Ohgon is said to be two individuals gained from hundreds of thousands of fry resulting from the crossing of the Kinbo and other strains of colored carp by the Sawato Aoki who lived at Takesawa Village in Niigata Prefecture in 1946.

**YAMABUKI OHGON** (yellow rose gold) (Below: Japanese Koi) (Right: German Carp.). This is a Ki Goi which has metallic sheen on the entire body. Unlike the original Ohgon, the color of this carp does not become blackish even when it undergoes environmental changes. Mr. Kataoka produced this carp as a result of the crossing of the Ki Goi and the Ohgon.

155

**SANSHOKU SHUSUI,** the Sanshoku autumn sky is a hybrid which resulted from a cross between a Taisho Sanshoku and a Shusui. It differs from the German (Doitsu) Sanshoku by the blue tinge on the dorsal edge. This color variety is very rare, so we had to be content with this poor specimen which needs much larger patches of black.

**NARUMI ASAGI** is the old name of the modern Asagi, which is a fish with the net-like pattern on the scales, red on the gill covers, pectoral fins and belly, and a white patch on the top of the head. This is a fine example except for the poor red patches.

**ASAGI,** one of the oldest of the Nishiki Goi (koi) color varieties, must have red on the opercula (gill covers), red on the pectoral fins, red on the belly, a white head and a very definite net-like pattern on the body caused by scales which have contrasting edges. The fish illustrated here has all of these characteristics . . . but it also has red on the dorsal fin which is a serious defect.

**ORANGE OHGON** (Above). This is an Ohgon with orange color and the scales are reticulated with a golden tint. In 1956, this was produced by crossing the Asagi and the Ohgon.

**NEZU OHGON** (silver gray gold) (Below). This is an Ohgon whose scales are reticulated with silver. The entire body is silver gray gold like tarnished silver. This is a carp of quiet and elegant hue.

**PLATINUM OHGON** (Upper: Japanese koi, lower: German carp). This is a Shiro Muji which has metallic sheen. This was produced from the crossing of the pink eyed Ki Goi (female) and the Nezu Ohgon (male) by Tadao Yaskioka who works at the Hokuriku Colored Carp Breeding Center. We now have very good specimens whose color is very clear and beautiful.

**TAKI ASAGI,** the waterfall Asagi, is a beautiful and rare color variety. The scales must be blue and so edged in contrasting white that the overall appearance is that of a shingled, mailed coat of armor. The Japanese liken this shingled effect to a waterfall, hence the name "waterfall Asagi." For years this fish was seen once in a million, now they are being cultivated in Minami Uwonuma District, Niigata Prefecture, Japan.

**GOSHIKI,** the five colored koi, is probably a hybrid which resulted from a cross between an Asagi and an Aka Bekko. The body has a very rare rust and purple color with indistinct flecking and bold red patches. Good specimens have a very deep red and very distinct purple tinges; this specimen is lacking in the purple. The five basic colors of this variety are white, red, black, brown, and where red and blue pigments mix, a purple tinge is shown.

**KIN SUI** (gold Shusui). This is another type of the Shusui with a metallic sheen as in the Ohgon. Unlike the Gin Sui, it has reddish color and is as beautiful as a brocade. It tends to lose its beauty when it grows older than two years of age. Masayuki Amano says that this was produced from the crossing of the Shusui and the Kin Kabuto (gold helmet).

162

**GIN SUI** (silver Shusui) is a Shusui with a metallic Ohgon sheen. It has glittering Ginrin (silverly glittering scales) with no red coloration. This fish type is said to lose its beauty when it grows older than two years of age.

**KINBO** is a Ma Goi koi or wild koi which has reticulated scales with golden tint along the dorsal fin only. This koi appears as a sport among the fry of the Ohgon. It has no commercial value.

**GINBO** (silver staff) is a Ma Goi (wild carp) whose dorsal area glitters silvery along the base of the dorsal fin. It has no commercial value.

**KINBO**

**GINBO**

163

**BUDO SANSHOKU** is a very colorful and attractive color variation of the Sanshoku which is intermediate between the Aigoromo and the Sumigoromo. It must have purple/red and white patches. This is an excellent specimen, as the colors are distinct and bright, especially the white and the clear white head. The shape of the fish is also extremely fine.

**AIGOROMO,** a hybrid produced by crossing an Asagi with a Kohaku, is characterized by a light blue tinge overlaying intensive red patches. The red patches must be uniformly placed along the back and each should have the blue overlay except the red patch on the top of the head. So perfect is this specimen that it has never lost any competition in this class (1973).

**KIN MATSUBA** (Matsuba Ohgon or Kinporai). This is a Matsuba with a metallic sheen like the Ohgon. The color ranges from light yellow to brown. Each scale glitters as if it were raised, and it makes a gorgeous impression in quiet patterns. It is said that it should glitter more clearly on rainy days.

**GIN MATSUBA** is another Matsuba with a metallic sheen. Unlike the Kin Matsuba, whose color ranges from thin yellow to brown, this koi has a silver tint.

**KIN KABUTO** (gold helmet) is an improved form of the Kinbo and has a gold helmet on the head with one golden streak along the dorsal fin from the shoulder to the caudal peduncle. The pectoral fins also glitter like gold.

**GIN KABUTO** (silver helmet) (Below) is an improved form of the Ginbo and has a silver helmet on the head with one silver streak along the back from the shoulder to the peduncle.

**SUMIGOROMO,** a hybrid produced by crossing an Asagi with a Kohaku, the same cross which produced the Aigoromo. This color variety, however, has black overlaying the red patches and it must have the black overlaying the head patch (whereas the Aigoromo could not have its head patch overlaid). This is a very beautiful fish with the basic three-stepped red pattern of intense coloration and deep coal black overlaid patches. Sumigoromo are much more rare than Aigoromo.

These two photographs are well worth comparing closely. The fish above is a Japanese carp or koi, and is fully scaled. The fish shown below is the German carp which is also called the "scaleless carp" or the "mirror carp." The top fish is known as Ohgon, or gold, and it covers the whole body. So metallic is the appearance of the scales that a visitor who sees one for the first time almost cannot believe his eyes. Sawata Awoki produced this fish in 1946. This specimen is superb since it has all the necessary qualities of a good Ohgon: a clean head, net-like scales all over the body (including the belly) and a long, slender body. This is the author's favorite fish which he kept for many years in New Jersey. The fish below is a Doitsu Nezu Ohgon, or German gray gold. Actually the fish is silver and is really referred to as Ibushi Gin which means "tarnished silver." This is an excellent specimen except for the horrible blemishes on the head.

Yamatonishiki

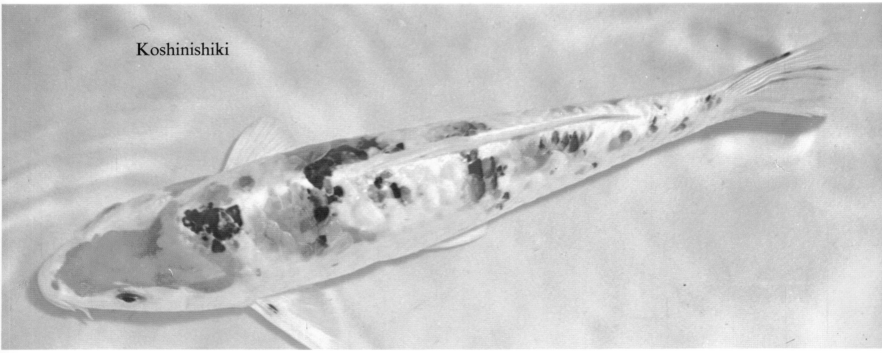

Koshinishiki

**YAMATONISHIKI** is a Taisho Sanshoku with silvery speckles on the head. The patterns are not distinctive and look rather vague. There are many points in this koi still to be improved.

**KOSHINISHIKI.** This carp is a variety of the Taisho Sanshoku with the tint of the Ohgon. At a glance, it looks like the Yamatonishiki.

170

**GIN-UTSURI** (silver reflection) is a Shiro-Utsuri with a metallic sheen. The metallic sheen is less dense than that of the Kin Ki-utsuri.

**KIN KI-UTSURI** (gold yellow reflection) is a Ki-utsuri with metallic sheen as the Ohgon. It has golden sheen on the head. Mr. Takahashi produced this carp in 1959 after many years of strenuous efforts.

**YAMBUKI OHGON,** the Yambuki gold, is a Kigoi or yellow carp which is named after the yellow rose, *Kerria japonica,* which the Japanese call "Yambuki." This fish was produced in 1957 by Seishu Kataoka of Higashiyama District, Niigata Prefecture. It is a hybrid produced from a Kigoi and an Ohgon.

**ORENJI OHGON,** or orange gold, was produced in 1956 by Seishu Kataoka by crossing the Ohgon and the Asagi. Because of its lack of lustre this is not a popular fish and it gets less attractive as it gets older. The very deep red Orenji Ohgon are called Hi Ohgon. "Orenji" is the way a Japanese would pronounce "orange" if he were to pronounce every letter in the word.

**PURACHINA OHGON,** the platinum koi, is a Shiro Muji which has a highly lustrous appearance. This variety was produced in 1963 by Tadao Yoshida of Uwotsu City, Toyama Prefecture, Japan. It is a hybrid which resulted from crossing an albino female Kigoi (yellow albino) with a male Nezu Ohgon. This is one of the few koi that breeds relatively true because of the pure albino strain which passes few, if any, color genes. Many top quality Purachina Ohgon koi are available and great emphasis is placed upon the beauty of the net-like scale pattern and the body conformation. The head is important; it must be totally free of imperfection.

**KIN SHOWA** is a Showa Sanshoku with a metallic sheen. The red does not become as deep and the metallic sheen fades as it grows old.

**GIN SHOWA** is a Showa Sanshoku with a silvery metallic sheen. This sheen tends to fade as it grows old.

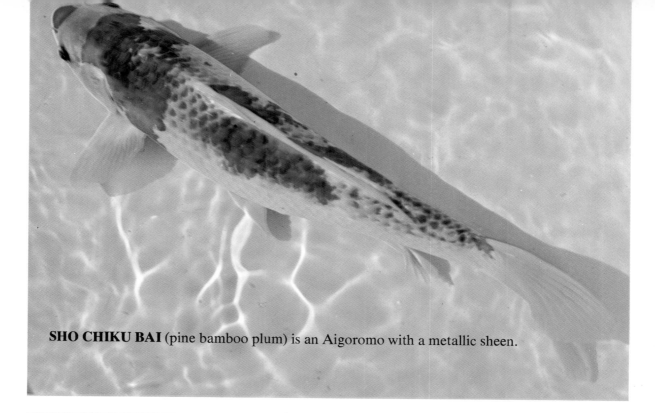

**SHO CHIKU BAI** (pine bamboo plum) is an Aigoromo with a metallic sheen.

**HI-OHGON** (Red Ohgon) is an Orange Ohgon whose orange color has become deep red.

**PLATINUM KOHAKU** (kin Fuji).

**KIN MATSUBA,** the gold pine needle koi, is a beautiful Matsuba with a highly lustrous metallic sheen. A darker, more brown variety is also available and is called "Kinporai." This is a common variety and great emphasis is placed upon body conformation and perfect net-like scalation patterns. The fish shown above has an almost perfect unblemished head.

**GIN MATSUBA,** the silver pine needle koi, is a silver Matsuba with a highly lustrous metallic sheen. Deep platinum coloration and excellence of the net-like scale pattern are mandatory in good specimens. The fish shown above has a very clean head.

**KIKU SUI** is another strain of the Shusui which has a metallic sheen. The color is basically like that of the platinum and in the ventral area it has waving patterns of orange or yellow rose.

**YAMABUKI HARIWAKE** (Japanese carp) is a Yamabuki Ohgon whose color is blended with the platinum Ohgon.

**HYAKUNENSAKURA.** This is a Kiku Sui whose dorsal area glitters.

**YAMABUKI HARIWAKE** (German carp).

**ORANGE HARIWAKE** is an Orange Ohgon whose color is blended with the platinum Ohgon.

**YAMATONISHIKI** is a Taisho Sanshoku with high lustre. Breeders are striving to produce this variety with a deeper red, similar to that seen in the Taisho Sanshoku. This is hardly a prize specimen in the illustration above, because it lacks the depth and magnitude of its black markings; the red patches are equally as inferior.

**KOSHINISHIKI** is a hybrid produced by crossing the Ohgon and the Taisho Sanshoku. It is often confused with the Yamatonishiki. Of the two specimens shown here, the one with the larger head patch of red is the better specimen, since it is more fully marked.

**KINSUI,** the golden Shusui, has German type scalation and a beautiful brocade design. Unfortunately, as this fish gets older it loses much of its color. Kaheiji Suda of Yamakoshi Village, Niigata Prefecture, Japan produced this hybrid in 1955 by crossing a Shusui with a Kin Kabuto. This specimen has an excellent head pattern and good body conformation.

**GINSUI,** the silver Shusui, has a Ginrin lustre without any red patches. It has excellent German scales and a nice blue cast to the basic body color, and the scales along the back are fairly uniform.

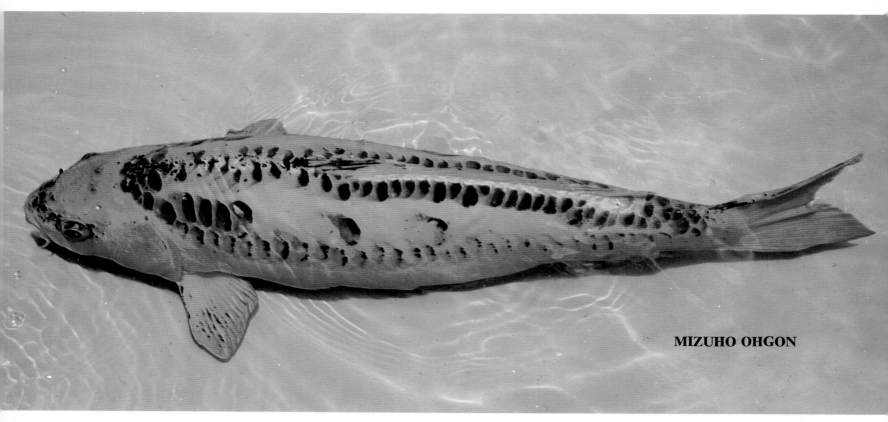

**MIZUHO OHGON**

**SAKURA OHGON**

**MIZUHO OHGON** is an Orange Ohgon with the scales of a mirror carp. The scales along the dorsal fin have a blackish metallic sheen. "Mizuho" is an ancient name of Japan and its meaning is the ear of rice plants and the Mizuho no Kuni (Japan) means a country with a big harvest of rice.

**SAKURA OHGON** is a variety of the Ohgon which has red markings like the Kanoko Kohaku.

**BENIKUJAKU**

**KUJAKU OHGON**

**BENIKUJAKU** (red peacock) is a variety of the Kujaku Ohgon (peacock Ohgon) whose red patches cover not only the head but also the entire body.

**KUJAKU OHGON** (peacock gold) is a Goshiki (five colors) with a metallic sheen. This is said to have been produced from crossing a female Shusui and a male Hariwake Ohgon.

**KIN KI-UTSURI,** the golden yellow reflection koi, is a Ki-utsuri with a highly lustrous coloration. The fish shown is very poor in quality since the standard calls for an unblemished red head. This strain was produced by Tozo Takahashi in Yamakoshi Village, Niigata Prefecture, Japan. The author has never seen a good specimen with a clear red head. Due to its shaded scales it might be better to call this variety "Kin Kage Utsuri."

**GIN UTSURI or KIN SHIRO UTSURI** is a Shiro Utsuri having a highly lustrous body but with a lighter golden shade than Kin Ki-utsuri. The deep black patches on the fish shown here is excellent but there is too much black on the pectorals and there are too many black imperfections on the lighter areas.

**GIN SHOWA,** the silver Showa, is a Showa with silver lustre which has been improved by inbreeding with a Purachina Ohgon to produce a platinum shading. This strain still requires improvement in deeper red and black.

185

**KARASU GOI** (crow) is a black carp which is often obtained as a sport from Konjo Asagi.

**HAJIRO** (white fins) is a Karasu Goi with white pectoral fins.

**YOTSUJIRO** (four white areas) is a Karasu Goi whose head, pectoral fins and caudal fin are white. This is sometimes called "Fuji Nishiki."

**HAGESHIRO** (patches of white) is a Karasu Goi whose snout and head have turned white.

187

**KIN SHOWA,** the golden Showa, is not a perfected strain as yet. The fish should have a golden lustre instead of the silver lustre shown on the fish illustrated above. This fish should really be called a "Gin Showa." The shape of the black patch on the head, mask-like in conformation, is ideal, and the beautiful pectoral fins have a very desirable Motoguro.

**SHO CHIKU BAI,** (top fish) the pine bamboo plum koi, is a truly Japanese favorite for it is named after the Pine Tree (Sho), the Chiku (Bamboo) and the Plum Tree (Bai), the most auspicious trees in Japan. This strain is an Aigoromo with high lustre. The lower photograph shows a HI OHGON, the red Ohgon, which is a deeper Orenji ( orange) Ohgon. The engraving shows the fish too light in red coloration to be truly considered a Hi Ohgon. This color variety is rare nowadays because of the popularity of the Purachina Ohgon and the Yamabuki Ohgon.

**SUMINAGASHI.**
This carp is basically black and has shaded patterns as if black ink were flushed in the water. Dr. Yoshiichi Matsui says that this carp is rare. The carp in the picture is a color variety of the Suminagashi which may well be called "Asagi Suminagashi."

**SUMINAGASHI**

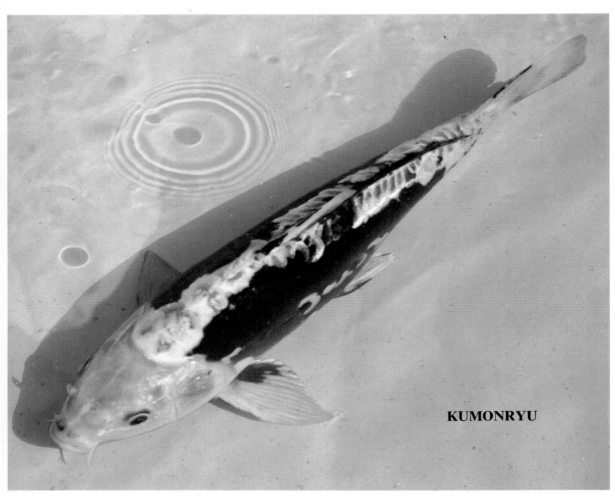

**KUMONRYU**
(dragon) is a Hageshiro whose white patches interlace the entire body. The name "Kumonryu" (dragon) is derived from the pattern it has on the dorsal area. The impression of the pattern is like that of a black and white painting which changes colors several times in a year. That is, the black patch changes into the white patch and vice versa.

**KUMONRYU**

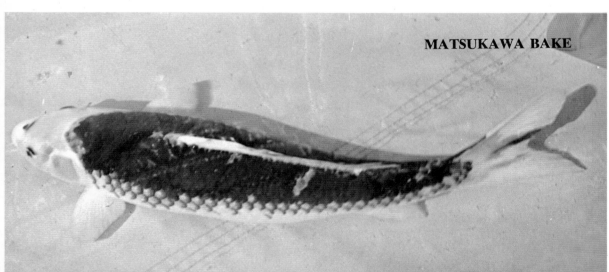

**MATSUKAWA BAKE**

**MATSUKAWA BAKE** is a variety of the Yotsujiro and the color combination of black and white is said to change several times in a year. That is, the black patch changes into the white patch and vice versa.

190

KI GOI

CHA GOI

**KI GOI** (yellow carp) is a yellow carp whose color tint ranges from orange to yellow. This is rarely produced from the fry of the Asagi, but those which are produced from these are liable to be pale in their yellow tint. The present Ki Goi are said to have been produced from the crossing of these and the Kohaku.

**CHA GOI** (brown carp) is a brownish saffron colored carp. It grows fast and soon becomes a large specimen.

**KIKUSUI** is an orange Hariwake Ohgon of the Doitsu type. It features a high platinum lustre on the back and rows of wavy red patches. The fish shown here is excellent because of its beautiful conformation of body, the almost perfect round red mark on the head and the full wavy red markings on each side of the dorsal edges. The pectoral fins are almost perfectly shaped.

**PURACHINA KOHAKU** or **KIN FUJI** is a platinum Ohgon with red patches which come from its Kohaku ancestry. According to Masayuki Amono, a Japanese authority on this breed, there are no more than 15 good fish produced from 10,000,000 fry! The specimen illustrated above is far from exceptional because its red patches are so weak.

**AKA MATSUBA** (red pine needle). The main color is dark brown with small black speckles scattered all over the body. If the red is clear and deep, the specimen is highly valued.

**KI MATSUBA** (yellow pine needle) is a variety of the Asagi. The main color is yellow and blue speckles are scattered in the reticulated scales on the dorsal edge.

**KI MATSUBA**
Japanese Carp

**KI MATSUBA**
German Carp

194

**AIGOROMO SANSHOKU** is a variety of the Taisho Sanshoku whose red patches contain blue speckles.

**KINSHU** (embroidered brocade). This was obtained as a by-product when the Koshi no Hisoku was produced. It is beautifully colored with red, green and golden tints as if it were brocaded.

195

**YAMABUKI HARIWAKE** shows mixtures of characteristics from both the Yamabuki and the Purachina Ohgon. There are many color varieties, but the Yamabuki areas must be large and the head must be completely platinum without any blemishes. This specimen is faulty because the Yamabuki patches are too spread out and too weak in color intensity; but the head is clear and beautiful.

**ORENJI HARIWAKE** is a conglomerate of the characteristics of the Orenji and Purachina Ohgon. The orange color in koi usually intensifies as the fish get older and larger, while the platinum areas usually atrophy. In the specimen shown above the platinum patches on the dorsal edge are too small and the contrast between the two colors is poor. This is not a good example or Orenji Hariwake.

**KOSHI NO HISOKU** (green carp). Green colored koi were produced by Tadao Yoshioka, as a result of crossing a female of the Shusui strain with a male of the Yamabuki Ohgon. Its main color is green, and the scales along the dorsal part have a golden sheen or silvery luster.

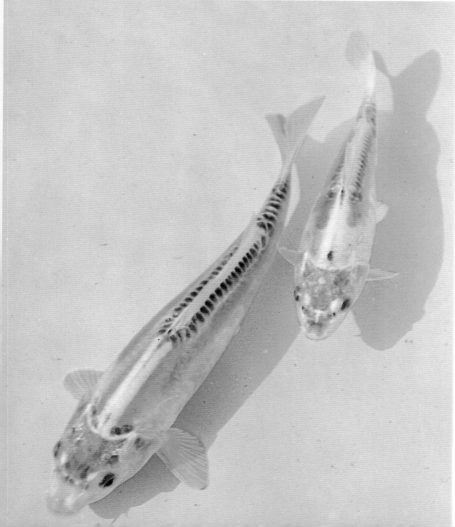

**HAKUSHU** is a hybrid of the Zuiun and the platinum Ohgon. It looks like the Nezu Ohgon, but unlike the Nezu Ohgon, it shows no fading of glittering even when the temperature makes considerable changes.

198

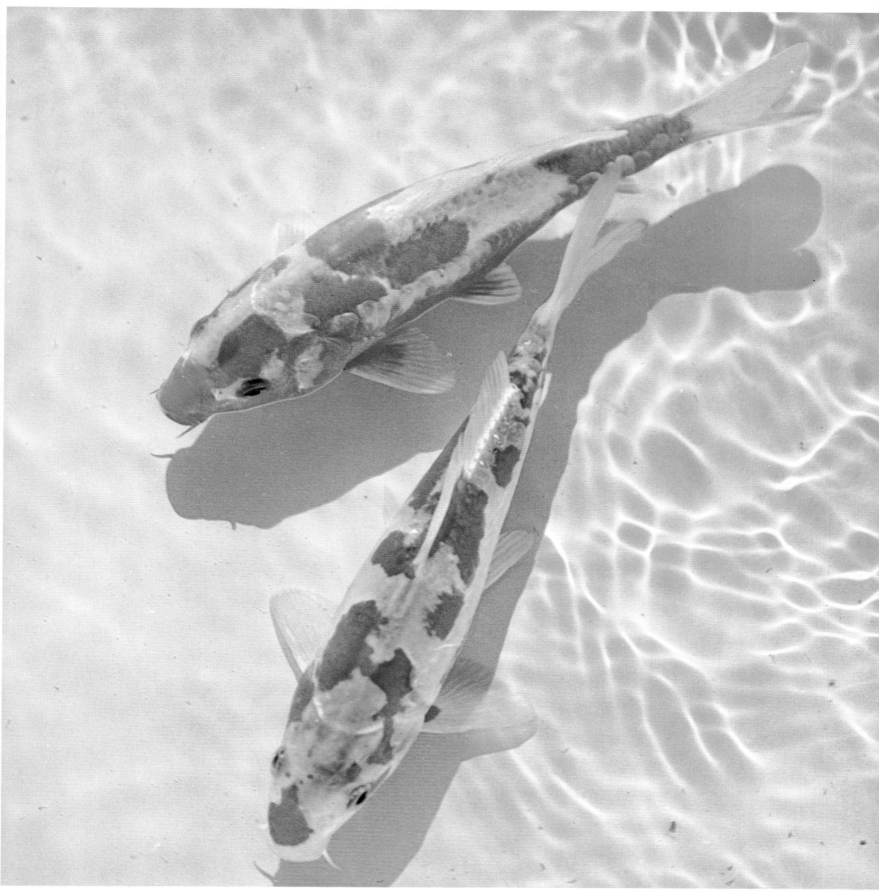

**ENYU** (voluptuous beauty). This was produced from the same parents as the Raigo. The Raigo and the Enyu are brothers and sisters of each other.

**MIZUHO OHGON** is a Orenji Ohgon of the German type (Doitsu). It must have lustrous black scalation with black being found only on the scales. This poor specimen has black blemishes on the head and body; the ugly distorted rays in the pectoral would make this fish better on a dinner plate than in a show ring.

**SAKURA OHGON,** above, the cherry blossom golden koi, is a Kanoko Kohaku with a high lustre. It should show some red Kanoko markings on a snow white background. This is an extremely rare variety and good specimens are hard to find. The fish shown above happens to be an excellent example of this variety. Its head is free of blemishes and the red on the paired fins, plus the enchanting red on the snout, makes this a winner.

**KUJAKU OHGON,** below, the peacock golden koi, is a Goshiki with high lustre and with red patches decorating the head. This strain was produced by Toshio Hirasawa in Minami Nigoro, Ojiya City, Niigata Prefecture, Japan in 1962 when he crossed a female Shusui with a male Hariwake Ohgon. The Doitsu (German) koi are very similar to the Kinsui. The fish shown below has a nice red head patch and a beautiful arrangement of the dorsal scales, but the head and body show intrusions of color.

**RAIGO** (sunrise viewed on a mountain top). In 1966, this was produced as a result of crossing a female Koshi no Hisoku with a male Zuiun. Greenish patches are seen in relief on the blue purplish body.

**ZUIUN** (auspicious clouds). In 1965, Mr. Yoshioka produced this carp as a result of crossing a female green carp with a male Shusui. Its color is bluish purple instead of the blue of the Shusui.

**SHIRO BEKKO GINRIN** is a Shiro Bekko with rows of Ginrin (silverly glittering scales) on the dorsal edge. It is highly valued as an elegant carp.

**TAISHO SANSHOKU GINRIN** is a Taisho Sanshoku with Ginrin (silverly glittering scales). When the Taisho Sanshoku has Ginrin, its red and black patches are liable to be pale or light. When these colors are well arranged and the shades are solid, it never fails to be a very charming carp as its beauty is well enhanced with its Ginrin.

**KARASU GOI,** the crow carp, originated from the Konjyo Asagi, which is a Prussian blue Asagi. It is strictly a black fish, but not intense coal black. The general appearance must be a velvety covering and the larger they are, the better.

**HAJIRO,** the white finned koi, is a Karasu which has white pectoral fins. The Japanese word "Ha" means wing, and the pectoral fins of fishes have always been compared to the wings of a bird; "Jiro" is another Japanese word meaning white. A perfect specimen would be completely black over its entire body and only the fins should have white with a Motoguro pattern decorating them. The specimen shown in this photo has white coloration on the body and does not have a Motoguro pattern on the pectorals. These defects are serious in this color strain.

**TANCHO SANSHOKU GINRIN**

**SHIRO UTSURI GINRIN**

**TANCHO SANSHOKU GINRIN.** The red patch on this carp is only situated on the head as in the Tancho. Rows of Ginrin are seen along the dorsal edge.

**SHIRO UTSURI GINRIN** is a Shiro Utsuri (white reflection) with Ginrin.

**KOHAKU GINRIN** is a Kohaku whose white scales are dotted with rows of silver glittering scales.

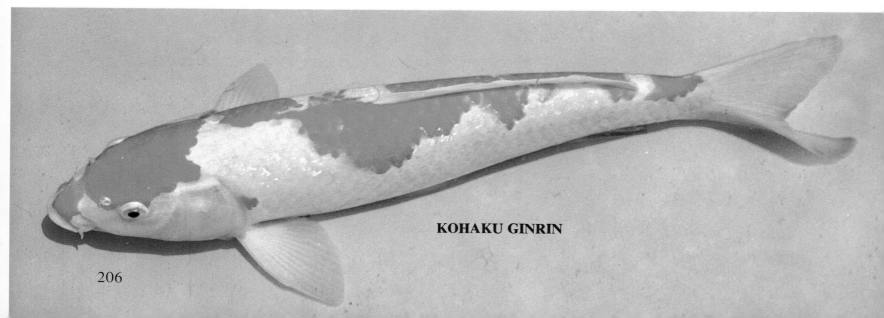

**KOHAKU GINRIN**

KAWA GOI

YOROI DOITSU

**KAWA GOI** (leather carp). This was imported from Germany in 1904. It has rows of large scales along the dorsal edge and no scales on the other parts of the body. The picture shows a Ki Goi (yellow carp) with typical scalation of the leather carp.

**YOROI DOITSU** (armor). This may be a mutant of the German carp with the large scales typical of the German carp covering the entire body, giving the carp an appearance of being armored. The picture shows Cha Goi (brown carp) with scales of the Yoroi Doitsu.

**YOTSUJIRO** is a koi with four white parts. It is basically a Karasu Goi whose head, tail and pectoral wings must be white. This specimen is defective because the back part of the fish is white and it should be black. In perfect specimens the four parts (head, two pectoral fins and tail) must be snow white.

**HAGEJIRO** or **KAMUROJIRO** is a variety of the Karasu Goi which has both head and fins which are white. This is not a good example of this strain because of the black on the head.

**SUMINAGASHI** is a black carp which exhibits the very desirable net-like pattern over the scales. This is a very rare color variety and one which is highly prized.

**KAGAMI GOI** (mirror carp). This is another type of German carp which was imported in 1904. It has rows of large scales not only along the dorsal fin but also along the lateral line. Very rare specimens have transparent scales. The picture shows a Nezu Ohgon with the typical scale pattern of the mirror carp.

**THE OLDEST CARP IN JAPAN (HANAKO).** This red carp enjoys the greatest longevity of carp in Japan. It is called by the pet name of 'Hanako,' which means 'Flower maid.'

**KAGAMI GOI,** or mirror carp, are a very old and familiar variety having been sold for many years in countries all over the world. In a good specimen the large scales must be neatly arranged in strict patterns as in the specimen shown in the photograph above. Both dorsal scales and lateral line scales are necessary. The fish in the photograph is called "Nezu Ohgon Doitsu Goi" and has superb scalation.

**KUMONRYU,** the dragon koi, is a Kamurojiro with white patches which should extend across the body appearing as a dragon drawn in black and white. The Japanese have an art they refer to as Sumi-e; this art is always black and white. This variety was described by Shinji Hoshino or Higashiyama, Niigata Prefecture, Japan in 1930. This is a German (Doitsu) type and exhibits metallic, lustrous white patches.

**MATSUKA BAKE** is a color variety of the Yotsujiro with black and white areas which change several times a year. The fish shown in the photograph above is in the middle of such a change and the white is becoming black. During the heat of the summer the fish becomes more white; during the winter the fish should be totally black.

**KI MATSUBA** is a variety of Asagi which has blue patches on the dorsal edges. The body must be golden yellow, not orange. It is very rare to see an excellent specimen. The fish shown in the photograph above is the German (Doitsu) type and has an Ohgon kind of lustre much like Kin Matsuba.

**AIGOROMO SANSHOKU** is a hybrid resulting from crossing a good Aigoromo and a Taisho Sanshoku. It must have blue splatterings on the red patches as well as deep black patches. The fish shown in the photograph above has excellent red, blue and black coloration, and its beauty is enhanced by the streaks in the pectoral fins.

**ETSU NO HISOKU,** the green carp, is a color variety produced by Tadao Yoshioka in Uwotsu City, Toyama Prefecture, Japan in 1965. The crossing of a female Shusui and a male Yamabuki Ohgon produced this beautiful color variety. The fish is primarily green with dorsal scales of a metallic golden or platinum lustre. The Governor of Toyama Prefecture gave the fish its Japanese name in 1966. "Etsu" is the name of an old Chinese country from ancient times; "Hisoku" refers to a very old type of chinaware which was always green in color.

**EN-YU** is a new variety which appeared on the scene in 1966. It was produced by Tadao Yoshioka, the famous Japanese koi breeder of Uwotsu City, by crossing a female Koshi no Hisoku with a male Shusui. It has a very bright over-all appearance with delicate, peaceful shadings and color patterns.

**KIN GIN RIN variety known as TAISHO SANSHOKU GINRIN.** This fish has Ginrin which is a silvery metallic scale pattern strewn haphazardly over the fish's body. The red and black patches should be light and small. The fish shown in the photograph above has excellent red patches and Ginrin over the dorsal scales. The high quality of its body conformation and its pectoral fins makes this an exceptionally fine specimen.

**SHIRO BEKKO GINRIN** has black patches which are usually light and small, as shown by the fish in the photograph above. The metallic scales are beautiful and this subtle beauty is very much appreciated by the Japanese.

**TANCHO KOHAKU GINRIN** has a smooth white appearance and an excellent pattern of Ginrin (metallic scales with a high sheen) along the lateral line. The red patch on the head is absolutely outstanding in color and shape and with the excellent body conformation makes this a champion quality fish.

**KAWA GOI,** the leather carp, is a Doitsu (German) carp which originated in Germany in the late 19th Century. It came to Japan in 1904 and was later crossed with an albino Kigoi and an Ohgon. Leather carp must have as few scales as possible. The few scales along the dorsal edge are tolerated.

**KIGOI,** the yellow carp, is a sport which appears among the millions of Asagi bred in Japan every year. It often becomes soiled with white or pink as it gets older. The new Kigoi were improved when they crossed the old Kigoi with Kohaku. Many albinos show up in this variety with pink eyes and they are known as Akame Kigoi which means "pink-eyed yellow carp."

**CHAGOI** are brown carp and the specimen shown here is a cull of Ohgon. This variety is very fast growing and would make a good food fish strain. The fish shown below has a very full body and nicely arranged mirror carp scales.

**AKA MATSUBA,** the red pine needle koi, is a color variation within the Matsuba strain. The whole body is red and some light black scales extend over the body giving a dark brown appearance to the reticulated pattern so desirable in all koi. The general appearance of the skin should be that of a pine cone. The fish in the accompanying photograph has a magnificent net-like pattern but the red color is not intense enough for it to be considered of championship quality.

**YOROI DOITSU,** the armored German carp, is not a popular variety in Japan, but it is favored in Germany. The Japanese claim the fish looks too warrior-like with its armor and is too disorganized and irregular in its appearance. The specimen in the photograph is called "Chagoi Yoroi Doitsu" or "brown armored German carp." Carp are important food fish in central Europe and many were raised for their coloration and scalation as well.

## PONDS

There are as many different kinds of ponds for your koi as there are different kinds of gardens. It hardly seems necessary to try to describe in words that which can be shown in photographs, so I have selected some of the most typical and beautiful ponds I could find in Hawaii and Japan and have reproduced them here for you to refer to or copy.

# INDEX

The following index is alphabetized according to the phonetic spelling of the Japanese language. There are many ways to spell Japanese words in English, and we have liberally used the various ways throughout the book. Thus you will find the word "Orange" spelled as "Orenji" as well as "Orange," because the Japanese spell it two ways. The same is true for certain Japanese words like "Sakura," which means "Cherry Blossom." It may also be spelled "Zakura." Even the word "Koi" is often spelled "Goi," so you can appreciate the problems of preparing this index. What the author has done is to use the spelling and name of the fish which was listed in the original competition in which the fish was entered. Thus there might not be consistency even where the same fish is involved.

Japanese name their carp along three basic lines. The most important method is to name the carp after its color. Another method is to name the fish after their analagous or similar popular object. Thus some koi are named after trees, flowers, birds and even sunsets and mountains. A final method of naming koi is derived from the city, district or even the name of the Empire. Thus "Showa" koi are named for the "Showa" dynasty, which is the present dynasty.

While the author has tried to translate the names as best he could, it can be understood that certain Japanese names are untranslatable, such as "Taisho" koi, many of which were not even produced in the Taisho era.